# Surviving Change:
# A Manager's Guide

# Surviving Change: A Manager's Guide

## Essential Strategies for Managing in a Downturn

Harvard Business School Press | *Boston, Massachusetts*

Copyright 2009 Harvard Business School Publishing
All rights reserved
Printed in the United States of America
Content in this book was previously published in *Harvard Business Essentials:
Managing Change and Transition* and *Harvard Business Essentials: Crisis
Management*

13  12  11  10  09      5  4  3  2  1

**Library of Congress Cataloging-in-Publication Data**

Surviving change : a manager's guide.
    p. cm.
  ISBN 978-1-4221-2977-7 (pbk.)
  1.  Executive ability. 2.  Leadership. 3.  Crisis management.
  HD38.2.S87 2009
  658.4'09—dc22

2009010448

# Contents

# Surviving Change:
# A Manager's Guide

# Introduction

Plenty of books have been written about change management, but few have addressed the critical issue covered in this guide. A *crisis* is a change—either sudden or evolving—that results in an urgent problem that must be addressed immediately. For a business, a crisis is anything with the potential to cause sudden and serious damage to its employees, reputation, or bottom line. Certainly the current economic climate places many managers firmly in a position of managing through crisis.

When faced with a crisis, managers must act quickly to recognize its source, contain it, and eventually resolve it with the least amount of damage. In this sense crisis management is part of a larger system of organizational risk management that includes diversification and insurance. And though most people can surely recall a crisis situation at their or another organization, few managers actively plan for potential crises. Fewer still receive training in crisis management. Neither of those deficiencies should surprise us, because crisis management as a formal field of study and training is relatively new, emerging only over the past three decades. This book aims to remedy the situation by explaining the essentials of change as it relates to crisis management. It will not make you an expert, but it will give you a practical framework for coming to grips with change of all sorts—including mastering an unplanned and unanticipated damaging event.

Change is almost always disruptive and, at times, traumatic. Because of this, many people avoid it if they can. Nevertheless, change is part of organizational life and essential for progress. And it's unavoidable in these times of crisis. Those who know how to anticipate it, catalyze it, and manage it will make their careers, and their companies, more satisfying and successful.

In this book you will learn how to manage change in a crisis constructively, and how to help your company, division, and people deal with the upheavals of change. You'll also learn practical things you can do to make change initiatives more successful and less painful for the people you manage.

This book compiles the best information on this subject from Harvard Business Publishing. It takes the essential chapters from two previously published Harvard Business Essentials books—*Managing Change and Transition* and *Crisis Management*—and packages them here in a manageable, practical format. It provides essential information on the management of change in organizations, with examples from business, and with numerous practical tips to make your efforts more effective.

# 1

# The Dimensions of Change

## Examining the Different Types and Approaches

## Key Topics Covered in This Chapter

- *An overview of the primary types of change*

- *A discussion of two different approaches to change: "Theory E" (which aims to increase shareholder value) and "Theory O" (which is focused on improving organizational capabilities)*

- *An evaluation of which approach to change is best or most appropriate*

**B**EFORE GETTING INTO the details of managing change, it's useful to overview the types of change programs used by organizations and the different approaches to change that can be taken. This broad view will help you later as we get into the nitty-gritty of managing change.

## Types of Change

Organizations typically respond to the challenges of new technologies, new competitors, new markets, and demands for greater performance with various programs, each designed to overcome obstacles and enhance business performance. Generally, these programs fall into one of the following categories:

- **Structural change.** These programs treat the organization as a set of functional parts—the "machine" model. During structural change, top management, aided by consultants, attempts to reconfigure these parts to achieve greater overall performance. Mergers, acquisitions, consolidations, and divestiture of operating units are all examples of attempts at structural change.

- **Cost cutting.** Programs such as these focus on the elimination of nonessential activities or on other methods for squeezing costs out of operations. Activities and operations that get little scrutiny during profitable years draw the attention of cost cutters when times are tough.

- **Process change.** These programs focus on altering *how* things get done. You've probably been involved with one or more of these. Examples include reengineering a loan approval process, the company's approach to handling customer warranty claims, or even how decisions are made. Process change typically aims to make processes faster, more effective, more reliable, and/or less costly.

- **Cultural change.** These programs focus on the "human" side of the organization, such as a company's general approach to doing business or the relationship between its management and employees. A shift from command-and-control management to participative management is an example of cultural change, as is any effort to reorient a company from an inwardly focused "product push" mentality to an outward-looking customer focus.

None of these change programs are easy, nor is success ever assured. A structural change—such as the acquisition of a complementary business—might appear easy, since the entire deal can be handled by a small platoon of senior managers and consultants, with input from the board of directors. But such an operation results in a need for more amorphous changes, such as eliminating redundancies and getting the acquired units to work together smoothly, which can be enormously difficult and time-consuming. And the record shows that few of these initiatives come close to meeting the expectations of their supporters. On the other hand, a change that focuses on a discrete operation, such as improving the customer service function, may be both easier to handle and more likely to succeed, since it involves a small activity set. The employees involved in that function may be able to handle the job by themselves, perhaps with a bit of coaching from a knowledgeable consultant.

If your organization is contemplating a change program, it will be helpful to determine which of the categories described above the initiative falls into, and to predict how is it likely to affect the overall company. Envisioning potential stumbling blocks in advance could prevent difficult issues from arising during the change process, and help ensure the success of the operation.

## Two Different Approaches to Change

While there are many types of change programs, two very different goals typically drive a change initiative: *near-term economic improvement* or an *improvement in organizational capabilities*. Harvard Business School professors Michael Beer and Nitin Nohria coined the terms "Theory E" and "Theory O" to describe these two basic goals.[1]

### Theory E: An Economic Approach

The explicit goal of Theory E change is to dramatically and rapidly increase shareholder value, as measured by improved cash flow and share price. Popular notions of employee participation and the "learning organization" take a back seat to this overarching goal. Financial crisis is usually the trigger for this approach to change. Driven to increase shareholder value, Theory E proponents rely heavily on mechanisms likely to increase short-term cash flow and share price: performance bonuses, headcount reductions, asset sales, and strategic reordering of business units. Jack Welch's 25 percent headcount reduction at GE, and his subsequent "be #1 or #2 in your market or be sold" strategy are prime examples of actions stemming from a Theory E change process.

According to Theory E, all implicit contracts between the company and its employees, such as lifetime employment, are suspended during the change effort. Individuals and units whose activities fail to demonstrate tangible value creation—for example, corporate planning or R&D—are particularly vulnerable.

The CEO and the executive team drive Theory E change from the top. Corporate departments, operating units, and employees involved in this approach are like pieces on management's strategic chessboard; they are rearranged or combined, and occasionally cashed out. Outside consultants provide advice to members of the inner circle: strategy consultants help management identify and weigh its options; valuation specialists and investment bankers arrange for asset sales and/or acquisitions; and HR consultants help with thorny layoff issues.

## Theory O: An Organizational Capabilities Approach

We've all been told that the most successful and enduring organizations are those with dynamic, learning-oriented cultures and highly capable employees. Companies such as Intel, Microsoft, 3M, Schwab, and Merck come to mind. The goal of Theory O change is to develop an organizational culture that supports learning and a high-performance employee base.

Companies that follow this approach attempt to invigorate their cultures and capabilities through individual and organizational learning. And that requires high levels of employee participation, flatter organizational structure, and strong bonds between the organization and its people. Because employee commitment to change and improvement are vital for Theory O change to work, implicit contracts with employees are considered too important to break—quite the opposite from what happens in the Theory E organization. For example, when Hewlett-Packard found itself stagnating in the early 1980s, it didn't jettison people to cut costs; it reduced bureaucracy and gave people and operating units greater autonomy. That approach was consistent with HP's time-honored tradition of valuing its people assets above all others.

An organization that banks on its culture and people to drive financial success is potentially incompatible with concentrated power and direction from the top. But leaders of Theory O change are less interested in driving the success themselves than in encouraging participation within the ranks, and in fostering employee behaviors and attitudes that will sustain such change.

## Which Is Best—Or Most Appropriate?

If your organization is considering a major change program, you are probably wondering which is best. Unfortunately, the record shows that neither approach is a guarantee of success. Theory E, aiming for rapid improvements in profitability, often succeeds in the short run, but does so at the expense of future vitality. By decimating employee ranks, it leaves survivors demoralized and disloyal. Any commitment they had to the company and its goals evaporates. Ironically, the people the organization hopes to retain—the brightest and most marketable employees—are among the first to snap up severance packages and look for greener pastures.

Nor do Theory E's draconian measures always produce the desired results. A survey conducted after the last wave of corporate downsizings (late 1980s through early 1990s) found that only 45 percent of downsizers reported higher operating profits.[2]

Theory O is not an ideal solution either. Reorienting corporate culture around employee commitment and learning is a noble endeavor, but it is a multiyear proposition. A successful program may produce a smarter, more adaptive employee base in four to five years, but companies that really need change cannot wait that long for results. Managers and employees, not to mention analysts and shareholders, simply aren't that patient.

Most companies studied by Beer and Nohria eschewed both pure Theory E and Theory O as solutions, preferring a mix of the two to suit their needs. Indeed, this may be the best path for your organization to follow (see "A Tale of Two Theories" for examples of the pitfalls of attempting to apply only one of the approaches).

## A Tale of Two Theories

To illustrate Theory E and Theory O, Michael Beer and Nitin Nohria have described two companies in similar businesses that adopted almost pure forms of each archetype: Scott Paper used Theory E to enhance shareholder value, while Champion International used Theory O to achieve a cultural transformation aimed at increasing productivity and employee commitment. Here's how they described these initiatives to readers of the *Harvard Business Review*:

*When Al Dunlap assumed leadership of Scott Paper in May 1994, he immediately fired 11,000 employees and sold off several*

> *businesses. . . . As he said in one of his speeches: "Shareholders are the number one constituency. Show me an annual report that lists six of seven constituencies, and I'll show you a mismanaged company." From a shareholder's perspective, the results of Dunlap's actions were stunning. In just 20 months, he managed to triple shareholder returns as Scott's market value rose from about $3 billion in 1994 to about $9 billion in 1995. . . . Champion's reform effort couldn't have been more different. CEO Andrew Sigler acknowledged that enhanced economic value was an appropriate target for management, but he believed that goal would be best achieved by transforming the behaviors of management, unions, and workers alike.[a]*
>
> In the end, neither company achieved its goal. Dunlap was forced to sell a demoralized and ineffective organization to Kimberly-Clark, and a languishing Champion International was sold to UPM-Kymmene. These failures contrast sharply with the successes enjoyed by companies that skillfully integrated the two approaches.

[a] Michael Beer and Nitin Nohria, "Cracking the Code of Change," *Harvard Business Review* 78, no. 3 (May–June 2000): 135.

"Companies that effectively combine hard and soft approaches to change can reap big payoffs in profitability and productivity," the authors write. "Those companies are more likely to achieve a sustainable competitive advantage [and] . . . reduce the anxiety that grips whole societies in the face of corporate restructuring."[3] They offer General Electric as an example, where former CEO Jack Welch employed both approaches in turn. First he squeezed out all of the redundancies and under-performing units through draconian Theory E methods. He then followed with change initiatives designed to improve the competitiveness of the company's culture by making it faster, less bureaucratic, and more customer-focused—a Theory O move. As described by David Ulrich:

*By the late 1980s, GE was strategically strong, with thirteen major businesses, each lean, globally positioned, and number one or two in market share. Since the latter part of the 1980s, GE's management has focused on more fundamental culture change. Under the rubric Work-out, a number of initiatives involved GE employees in dismantling bureaucracies, making faster decisions, moving more quickly to serve customers, and getting rid of unnecessary work. Through town-hall meetings in which employees worked with managers to identify and eliminate unnecessary work, GE worked to incorporate the values of speed, simplicity, and self-confidence into the organization's culture.*[4]

In a sense, GE's method was to fix the "hardware" first through divestitures and consolidations. Once that job was completed, it turned

**TABLE 1 - 1**

## Key Factors in Theory E and Theory O Change

| Dimensions of Change | Theory E | Theory O | Theories E and O Combined |
|---|---|---|---|
| Goals | Maximize shareholder value | Develop organizational capabilities | Embrace the paradox between economic value and organizational capability |
| Leadership | Manage change from the top | Encourage participation from the bottom up | Set direction from the top and engage the people below |
| Focus | Emphasize structure and systems | Build up corporate culture: employees' behavior and attitudes | Focus simultaneously on the hard (structures and systems) and the soft (corporate culture) |
| Process | Plan and establish programs | Experiment and evolve | Plan for spontaneity |
| Reward system | Motivate through financial incentives | Motivate through commitment—use pay as fair exchange | Use incentives to reinforce change but not to drive it |
| Use of consultants | Consultants analyze problems and shape solutions | Consultants support management in shaping their own solutions | Consultants are expert resources who empower employees |

*Source:* Michael Beer and Nitin Nohria, "Cracking the Code of Change," *Harvard Business Review* 78, no. 3 (May–June 2000): 137.

its focus to the "software"—its employees and how they conducted their work.

Which approach is best for your particular situation? Only the people who are familiar with the inner workings of your company can say with any authority. To help you think through the pros and cons of each theory, table 1-1 summarizes the two archetypal change approaches—and their combination—in terms of key factors. You can tell a lot about the mind-set of your company's executives by checking off how they manage each of the six factors.

## Summing Up

This chapter highlighted the different types of change initiatives observed in organizations:

- structural change

- cost cutting change

- process change

- and cultural change

It also explored two different approaches that can be taken to pursue these changes:

- Theory E change aims for a dramatic and rapid increase in shareholder value. It is driven from the top of the organization and makes heavy use of outside consultants. Theory E relies heavily on cost cutting, downsizing, and asset sales to meet its objectives.

- Theory O change aims to create higher performance by fostering a powerful culture and capable employees. It is characterized by high levels of employee participation and flatter organizational structure, and attempts to build bonds between the enterprise and its employees. Unlike Theory E, this approach to change is a long-term proposition.

# 2

# Seven Steps to Change

## A Systematic Approach

## Key Topics Covered in This Chapter

* *A description of a seven-step change process*

* *An explanation of the roles that leaders, managers, and HR play during this process*

* *Tips on mistakes to avoid during implementation*

I F Y O U ' V E B E E N around big corporations for any length of time, you have probably been on the receiving end of several change programs. Here's a typical scenario:

*All employees are assembled in the cafeteria where the CEO, flanked by the head of human resources and a consultant in a thousand-dollar suit, delivers a speech on yet another plan to make your company more productive and profitable. In years past, plans for quality circles, service excellence, a pay-for-performance system, and process reengineering were tried. Today it's The New Thing. The consultant then touts the virtues of this panacea, points to a handful of companies that have used it to revitalize their performance, and describes what it can do here. Eventually pizza is served and everyone goes back to work, muttering "Here we go again."*

If this little scenario sounds less than promising, let's speculate on some reasons why. If you had been in that audience, you'd probably be thinking:

"Why is this important?"

"What's in it for me?"

"How do these people know what the problems are? They haven't even bothered to ask *us*."

"Do they really think they can change the entire company at once?"

"How much of our time and their money will they sink into this dry hole?"

If this scenario seems overly contrived and pessimistic, consider this: In aggregate, the scorecard for change programs is very disappointing. By some estimates, 70 percent of change initiatives fail to meet their objectives.[1] As author John Kotter once put it, "If you were to grade them using the old fashioned A, B, C, D, and F, I'd be surprised if an impartial jury would give 10% of these efforts an A. But I'm not saying that 90% deserve a D either. What is tragic is that there are so many C-pluses. It's one thing to get a C-plus on a paper; it's another when millions of dollars or thousands of jobs are at stake."[2]

Clearly, organizations need to do better. And they can if they approach change with the right attitude, from the right angle, and with a solid set of action *steps*—which is what this chapter will offer.

## The Seven Steps

Back in 1990, Michael Beer and his colleagues Russell Eisenstat and Bert Spector identified a number of steps that general managers at business unit and plant levels could use to create real change. Those steps produced a self-reinforcing circle of commitment, coordination, and employee competency—all bedrocks of effective change.[3] Their steps have lost none of their potency over the years since their work was published, and so we will cover several of them here in detail. In addition, we add two others: one borrowed from General Electric's Management Development Center (step 3), and another suggested by Robert Schaffer and Harvey Thomson (step 4).

You can use these steps to guide your own change efforts.

### Step 1. Mobilize Energy and Commitment through Joint Identification of Business Problems and Their Solutions

The starting point of any effective change effort, according to Beer et al., is a clear definition of the business problem. Problem identification answers the most important question that affected personnel want to know: Why must we do this? The answer to this question can lay the foundation for motivation, and thus must be answered convincingly. The "why" of change may be a looming crisis, years of declining profit margins, or research that indicates that the public doesn't like doing business with your company.

Answering "why" is essential not just for its motivating potential, but also because it creates a sense of urgency, and, as we've discussed, change won't happen without urgency. People will not grapple with the pain and effort of serious change without a sense that "We have to do this—like it or not!"

How much urgency is required? Here's a good rule of thumb: Your change goals cannot be achieved unless 75 percent of managers are genuinely convinced that sticking with the status quo is more dangerous or more painful than striking out on another path.[4]

Though problem identification is a must, *how* the problem is identified is also important. Motivation and commitment to change are greatest when the people who will have to make the change and live with it are instrumental in *identifying the problem and planning its solution*. This is nothing more than common sense. Being involved in pinpointing the issue also assures the rank and file that the identified problem is the right one.

The idea that the people closest to a situation can identify the problem is something that senior executives and staff people sometimes fail to appreciate. People at the top often assume (wrongly) that they have identified the entire problem. The truth is that they generally understand *part* of the problem but fail to understand it *in toto*. Their top-down approach results in two serious errors: The problem is improperly defined, and the solution is too narrowly drawn. Either error can torpedo the change program. The same can happen when the CEO puts a consultant on the case. Consulting companies have a habit of creating solutions to problems and then peddling them like bottled medicine to organizations that appear to have the right symptoms. Unfortunately, unlike medicinal treatments, off-the-shelf business improvement solutions created by consultants are not subjected to rigorous testing. No objective testing by disinterested parties is done to determine their efficacy or the conditions under which they work or fail. There are no control groups, and no control of the many variables that affect success and failure. And there is no warning of possible "side effects." Nor does effectiveness in one operating unit assure effectiveness in others within the same company. So beware of cookie-cutter solutions.

Top-driven change also creates people problems. People resist having solutions imposed on them by individuals who lack intimate familiarity with their day-to-day operations. Their resistance is expressed through a lack of motivation and commitment to change. This is not to say that top management has no role to play in organizational change. It is generally their job to sound the warning that substantive change is needed, and their support for a change initiative is essential. As John Kotter has written: "[M]ajor change is impossible unless the head of the organization is an active supporter."[5] In his experience, successful transformation is supported by a coalition of key individuals that include the CEO, division general manager, and other leaders including, in some instances, a key customer or union official. But there is a big difference between top-level support and top-level control.

The second part of this step, after defining the business problem, is developing a solution to the problem. Here again employees should be involved. A good example of this was seen in the case of Philips, the Dutch electronics giant. In the early 1990s, newly appointed CEO Jan Timmer initiated a change program aimed at restoring the company's growth and profitability. He mobilized energy and commitment by generating a sense of urgency and by getting everyone involved. Though it began with the top one hundred executives, the Philips initiative cascaded to each succeeding level. As described in an article by Paul Strebel:

> *Timmer knew that he could not accomplish his goals unless managers and subordinates throughout the company were also committed to change. Employees' concerns about this corporate initiative had to be addressed. . . . At workshops and training programs, employees at all levels talked about the consequences and objectives of change. Timmer reached out via company "town meetings" to answer questions and talk about the future. His approach made people feel included, and his direct style encouraged them to support him. It soon became clear that employees were listening and the company was changing.*[6]

You can do something similar in your company or your unit. The first task is to bring people face-to-face with urgent business problems and their root causes. Then make sure they understand the possible consequences—in personal terms—if those problems are not solved: bonuses eliminated, layoffs, possible sale of the company, and so forth. Doing so will puncture any sense of complacency.

If waning profitability is the problem, hold a meeting in which the decline in profits is demonstrated graphically. Then involve people from different levels in ferreting out the causes of profit decline. Is lower revenue the problem, higher costs, or both? Ask them to dig farther and find the root causes. If higher costs are the cause of profit decline, which specific costs are on the rise—and why? How could those rising costs be reversed? (For more on identifying the business problem, see "Motivate by Finding Gaps.")

## Step 2. Develop a Shared Vision of How to Organize and Manage for Competitiveness

The people in charge of change must develop a clear vision of an altered and improved future. They must also be able to communicate that vision to others in ways that make the benefits of change clear. In communicating the vision, be very specific about how the change will: 1) improve the business (through greater customer satisfaction, product quality, sales revenues, or productivity), and 2) how those improvements will benefit employees. Employee benefits might include higher pay, larger bonuses, new opportunities for advancement, or greater job security.

Price Pritchett, a change management expert at Dallas-based Pritchett & Associates, says that 20 percent of employees tend to support a change from the start, another 50 percent are fence-sitters, and the remaining 30 percent tend to oppose the change. Those fence-sitters and resisters must be converted and enlisted to participate in realizing the vision. It isn't enough to just identify the problem and agree on how to proceed. You have to get people excited and involved.

An effective vision can get most employees on the side of change. But what constitutes an effective vision? John Kotter has suggested six characteristics. From his perspective, an effective vision must:[7]

## Motivate by Finding Gaps

Effecting meaningful change requires a clear understanding of current conditions and desired outcomes. By determining what is critical to the success of the organization in each of its core processes—for example, marketing, manufacturing, satisfying clients—and by detailing the desired future states, you and your team have an opportunity to identify any "gaps" in organizational performance. These gaps can be the basis for broad-based motivation to change.

### Xerox Discovers a Critical Cost Gap

In 1979, Xerox's copier division set out to benchmark its productivity measures against those of rising foreign competitors. Xerox had invented the copier industry, and virtually owned it until this time. But now Japanese companies were coming out with smaller, less expensive, and more reliable models. Xerox was aware of a substantial cost difference between their operations and those of these new competitors, but lacked the details.

Working through its Japanese partner, Fuji Xerox, the American company performed *gap analysis* to identify and measure what turned out to be a shocking cost gap. Its Japanese rivals were profitably selling their machines in the United States at less than Xerox's own cost of production! This was startling news. Once the gap was quantified, it became the centerpiece of a change initiative that introduced the quality and benchmarking techniques that successfully reformed Xerox.

1. describe a desirable future—one that people would be happy to have right now if they could;

2. be compelling—that is, it must be so much better than the current state that they will gladly undertake the effort and sacrifice as necessary to attain it;

3. be realistic—the vision must be perceived as being within the grasp of a hardworking group of people;

4. be focused—for example, it should limit itself to a manageable and coherent set of goals, such as six sigma quality, or customer service that resolves a customer's problem with a single phone call;

5. be flexible—that is, able to adapt to changing circumstances; and

6. be easy to communicate to different levels.

Two cautions about the "vision." First, a powerful vision can inspire and motivate. But a vision must be "translatable" by managers and employees into actions that will produce tangible results. So always ask: "What *specifically* should this vision produce?" It might be a 25 percent reduction in production rejects, a 20 percent profit improvement next year, or a loan approval decision in one day instead of three. Whatever it is for your organization, don't allow a lofty vision to crowd out specific improvement goals.

The second caution is to make the vision compatible with the core values of the organization—the values that have sustained it over the years. If a vision does not resonate with those values, the change process could invite conflicted behavior and confusion about what's the right thing to do.

### Step 3. Identify the Leadership

Be sure that you have a visible leader and sponsor of change, someone who owns and leads the change initiative. The leadership must act as champion, assemble the resources needed for the project, and take responsibility for success or failure. This is a step that General Electric insists on for its own change initiatives. What kinds of people are most suitable for change leadership? Successful change leaders, according to Beer, Eisenstat, and Spector, share three characteristics:[8]

1. They have a persistent belief that revitalization is key to competitiveness and a deep conviction that fundamental change will have a major impact on the bottom line—and they aren't shy about it.

2. They articulate their conviction in the form of a credible and compelling vision. People won't buy into the pain and effort of change unless they can see a future state that is tangibly better—and better for them—than the one they have at the moment. Successful change leaders can form such a vision and communicate it in compelling terms.

3. They have the people-skills and organizational know-how to implement their vision. This ability to get the job done, per Beer et al., is a function of operating experience. "Only those leaders with a depth of operating management experience seemed able to successfully implement their vision of a revitalized organization."[9] A lack of operating knowledge, according to their studies, fatally undermines an individual's ability to make change happen.

This last point contains a clear warning: As you identify leadership for change, don't be tempted to put the human resources department in charge. HR may be respected for its know-how in areas of personnel and benefits, but it is often seen as clueless about operations. The same goes for other staff functionaries. Again, control and responsibility must be situated in the units undergoing change, and handled by the unit leaders.

### Step 4. Focus on Results, Not on Activities

Many companies make the mistake of focusing measurement and managerial attention on training, team-creation, and other activities that—logically—should produce desirable results down the road. Per Robert Schaffer and Harvey Thomson's research, these activities "sound good, look good, and allow mangers to feel good," but contribute little or nothing to bottom-line performance.[10] They cite the example of one major enterprise that, after three years, proudly pointed to forty-eight improvement teams, high morale, and two completed quality improvement plans—but absolutely *no* measurable performance improvements!

As an antidote to activity-focused programs, Schaffer and Thomson recommend a shift to measurable short-term performance improvement goals, even though the change campaign is a long-term, sustained one. For example, "Within ninety days we will reduce fuel costs by 15 percent." Results-driven improvement efforts bypass lengthy periods of preparation, training course development, and other "rituals" of change. (See "Putting Results-Driven Change into Practice" for an expanded example of results-driven change.)

## Putting Results-Driven Change into Practice

Step 4 advocates a focus on results instead of a focus on activities. Here is an example of how one organization used that advice.

The Eddystone Generating Station of Philadelphia Electric, once the world's most efficient fossil-fuel plant, illustrates the successful shift from activity-centered to results-driven improvement. As Eddystone approached its thirtieth anniversary, its thermal efficiency—the amount of electricity produced from each ton of coal burned—had declined significantly. The problem was serious enough that top management was beginning to question the plant's continued operation.

The station's engineers had initiated many corrective actions, including installing a state-of-the-art computerized system to monitor furnace efficiency, upgrading plant equipment and materials, and developing written procedures for helping operating staff run the plant more efficiently. But because the innovations were not built into the day-to-day operating routine of the plant, thermal efficiency deteriorated whenever the engineers turned their attention elsewhere.

In September 1990, the superintendent of operations decided to take a results-driven approach to improve thermal efficiency. He and his management team committed to achieve a specific incremental improvement of thermal efficiency worth about $500,000 annually—*without* any additional plant investment. To get started, they identified a few improvements that they could accomplish within three months and established teams to tackle each one.

A five-person team of operators and maintenance employees and one supervisor took responsibility for reducing steam loss from hundreds of steam valves throughout the plant. The team members started by eliminating all the leaks in one area of the plant. Then they moved on to other areas. In the process, they invented improvements in valve-packing practices and devised new methods for reporting leaks. Another employee team was assigned the task of reducing heat that escaped through openings in the huge furnaces. For its first subproject, the group ensured that all ninety-six inspection doors on the furnace walls were operable and were closed when not in use. Still another team, this one committed to reducing the amount of unburned carbon that passed through the furnace, began by improving the operating effectiveness of the station's coal-pulverizer mills in order to improve the carbon burn rate.

Management charged each of these cross-functional teams not merely with studying and recommending but also with producing measurable results in a methodical, step-by-step fashion. A steering committee of station managers met every two weeks to review progress and help overcome obstacles. A variety of communication mechanisms built awareness of the project and its progress. For example, to launch the process, the steering committee piled two tons of coal in the station manager's parking space to dramatize the hourly cost of poor thermal efficiency. In a series of "town meetings" with all employees, managers explained the reason for the effort and how it would work. Newsletters reviewed progress on the projects—including the savings realized—and credited employees who had contributed to the effort.

As each team reached its goal, the steering committee, in consultation with supervisors and employees, identified the next series of performance improvement goals, such as the reduction

*Continued*

of the plant's own energy consumption, and commissioned a number of teams and individuals to implement a new round of projects. By the end of the first year, efficiency improvements were saving the company over $1 million a year, double the original goal.

Beyond the monetary gains—gains achieved with negligible investment—Eddystone's organizational structure began to change in profound ways. What had been a hierarchical, tradition-bound organization became more flexible and open to change. Setting and achieving ambitious short-term goals became part of the plant's regular routine as managers pushed decisions further and further down into the organization. Eventually, the station manager disbanded the steering committee, and now everyone who manages improvement projects reports directly to the senior management team. Eddystone managers and workers at all levels have invented a number of highly creative efficiency-improving processes. A change so profound could never have happened by sending all employees to team training classes and then telling them, "Now you are empowered; go to it."

In the course of accomplishing its results, Eddystone management introduced many of the techniques that promoters of activity-centered programs insist must be drilled into the organization for months or years before gains can be expected: employees received training in various analytical techniques; team-building exercises helped teams achieve their goals more quickly; teams introduced new performance measurements as they were needed; and managers analyzed and redesigned work processes. But unlike activity-centered programs, the results-driven work teams introduced innovations only if they could contribute to the realization of short-term goals. They did not inject innovations wholesale in the hope that they would somehow generate better results. There was never any doubt that responsibility for results was in the hands of accountable managers.

SOURCE:   Robert H. Schaffer and Harvey A. Thomson, "Successful Change Programs Begin with Results," *Harvard Business Review* 70, no. 1 (January–February 1992): 87–88.

### Step 5. Start Change at the Periphery, Then Let It Spread to Other Units without Pushing It from the Top

The likelihood of success is greatest when change is instigated in small, fairly autonomous units. Changing an entire organization at once is much more difficult and less likely to succeed. Once change on a smaller scale is accomplished and witnessed by employees in adjacent units, diffusion of the change initiative throughout the organization is much more likely.

SQA, an innovative unit of Herman Miller Company, a leading office furniture manufacturer, provides a powerful example of diffusion based on success in one unit. SQA, which stands for "simple, quick, affordable," was a fairly autonomous unit designed to serve the small businesses furniture market. Senior management gave this unit the freedom it needed to develop a new, faster, and low-cost approach to manufacturing and fulfillment. Personnel in that unit totally redesigned their furniture building process—from order-taking to delivery—basing it on digital connectivity, mass customization, and a new relationship with supply-chain partners. By the time the makeover was complete, SQA had cut the order-to-shipment cycle from eight weeks to less than one week. On-time shipments, a rarity in the industry, reached 99.6 percent. Better yet, revenue growth for SQA was outpacing the rest of Herman Miller, and its profit margins eclipsed not only those of the larger organization, but the furniture industry as a whole.[11]

Naturally, the parent company sought to emulate SQA's methods. To help things along, Herman Miller's top management promoted and "repotted" SQA managers and operations personnel into responsible positions elsewhere in the organization. From those positions, former SQA people were able to teach others about their fast, mass-customized, and on-time approach to manufacturing. They were positioned to motivate and guide change more broadly within the corporation.

Everett Rogers's work on the diffusion of innovation provides a useful guide to our expectations for the spread of change from one unit of an organization to another.[12] Per Rogers, we can expect a greater probability of success if the change contemplated has the following features:

- clear advantages over the status quo;

- compatibility with peoples' deeply-held values, experiences, and needs;

- requirements that are understandable;

- the option for people to experiment with the change model on a small scale; and

- the possibility for people to observe the result of the change in another setting.

Each of these characteristics, not surprisingly, applied to the SQA case.

### Step 6. Institutionalize Success through Formal Policies, Systems, and Structures

Getting an organization to change requires risk-taking and effort by many people. So once the objective is achieved, the last thing you want is for all your hard-earned gains to slip away. And they will if you don't take steps to prevent it. Gains can be consolidated and cemented through policies that describe how work is to be done, through information systems, and through new reporting relationships. For example, once it had achieved a key goal—over 99 percent on-time deliveries of furniture orders—SQA institutionalized its gains through a performance measurement system that kept everyone's focus on that metric. Everyone in the production facility, from the top to bottom, was expected to know the current level of on-time delivery, and various rewards were tied to it.

To follow through on the change process, it is critical that employees be as concerned with institutionalizing the "journey" as with implementing the process itself. *Continuous* improvement is the ultimate goal.

## Step 7. Monitor and Adjust Strategies in Response to Problems in the Change Process

Change programs almost never proceed according to plan. All types of unanticipated problems crop up as people move forward. Developments in the external environment can also affect what's going on inside the company. So change leaders must be flexible and adaptive, and their plans must be sufficiently robust to accommodate alterations in schedules, sequencing, and personnel.

To assess your organization's approach to change based on the seven steps outlined in this section, use table 2-1, "Self-Diagnosis."

---

TABLE 2 - 1

## Self-Diagnosis

*Now that you are acquainted with the seven steps of successful change, do a little diagnosis of your own organization. Consider how it has approached change in the past and how it is approaching any current initiatives. Then score it using this brief diagnostic test, using a 1–5 scale (1=strongly disagree, 5=strongly agree).*

| Our organization . . . | Score |
| --- | --- |
| Mobilizes energy and commitment to change through joint diagnosis of business problems | _____ |
| Develops a shared vision of how to organize and manage for competitiveness | _____ |
| Identifies leadership | _____ |
| Focuses on results, not on activities | _____ |
| Spreads change to other units without pushing it from the top | _____ |
| Institutionalizes success through formal policies, systems, and structures | _____ |
| Monitors and adjusts strategies in response to problems in the change process | _____ |

*How does your organization fare on these parameters? A score of three or less in any category points to serious weaknesses that you'll want to identify and correct.*

## Roles for Leaders, Managers, and HR

By definition, leaders create an appealing vision of the future and then develop a logical strategy for making it a reality. They also motivate people to pursue the vision, even in the face of obstacles. Managers, on the other hand, have the job of making complex tasks run smoothly. They have to work out the implementation details, round up the required resources, and keep employee energy channeled in the right direction. While leaders create a vision and plan for extending the train tracks into new territory, managers get the tracks built and make sure that the trains run on time. Thus, it is clear why the seven steps of change outlined here require effective leaders *and* managers, at all levels of the organization.

The distinction between leaders and managers, of course, is fuzzy and often arbitrary in practice. An effective leader always needs managerial skills, and every competent manager provides leadership to his or her direct reports. To evaluate your own effectiveness as a leader, it might be helpful to take the self-diagnostic test found in appendix A.

John Kotter has described the relationship of leadership and management in a simple two-by-two matrix, shown in figure 2-1. Here we see that transformation goes nowhere when both leadership and management are found wanting. Good short-term results are feasible when *either* effective leadership *or* effective managers are involved. But to enjoy long-term transformation success, both must be present.

HR professionals also have an important role to play in the success of change initiatives. We stated earlier that putting human resource personnel in charge of a change program simply paves the way to failure. Line operators—and not staff people from HR or other support functions—must lead the way within their own units. HR people, however, can play a critical supportive role by:

- helping management with the hiring and assignment of consultants;

- reassigning and/or outplacing personnel displaced by change;

**FIGURE 2-1**

## The Relationship of Leadership and Management

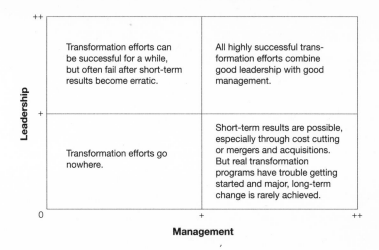

| | |
|---|---|
| Transformation efforts can be successful for a while, but often fail after short-term results become erratic. | All highly successful transformation efforts combine good leadership with good management. |
| Transformation efforts go nowhere. | Short-term results are possible, especially through cost cutting or mergers and acquisitions. But real transformation programs have trouble getting started and major, long-term change is rarely achieved. |

*Source:* John P. Kotter, *Leading Change* (Boston, MA: Harvard Business School Press, 1996), 129.

- arranging for employee training;

- facilitating meetings and off-site conferences; and

- helping institutionalize successful change through employee development, rewards, and organizational design.

Leaders, managers, and HR must all understand their unique role in a change process and play together as part of a team. In addition, each must recognize the critical role of rank and file employees, who must be active throughout the change effort.

## Mistakes to Avoid

It is possible to get halfway to success in your change initiative by simply avoiding common mistakes:

- **Don't try to impose a canned solution developed somewhere else.** Instead, develop the solution within the unit that needs change.

- **Don't place your bets on a companywide solution driven from the top.** There are some instances where this has worked, but usually only in cases where the company was heading down the tubes—and everyone knew it. If the company is large, the odds of changing an entire business in a single masterstroke are slim. Make the solution specific to the unit or units that need change.

- **Don't put HR in charge.** Put responsibility on the shoulders of unit leaders, and let them run their own show—with top management support.

- **Don't bank on a technical fix alone.** Businesses are social systems, not machines. To be effective, a technical fix must fit comfortably within the social fabric of the workplace, otherwise the workplace's immune system will attack it. Technical solutions usually miss the root causes of problems and fail to deal with the attitudes, skills, and motivations associated with them. In one classic case, a mining company's engineering solution to production efficiency was technically superior, but inadvertently broke up employee groups that had learned to work together and to support each other in a dangerous environment. The miners resisted the technical solution because it failed to account for how they worked together.

- **Don't attempt to change everything at once.** The biggest error of top-driven programmatic change is that it tries to do too much at once. Unless the entire organization is in crisis, begin change at the periphery, in units far from corporate headquarters, where local managers and their people can run the show and maintain control. That's what happened at Herman Miller, where the substantive change initially took place in its small operating unit, SQA. It's unlikely that the same success would have been achieved had Herman Miller tried to change everything in every one of its operating units in a bold stroke.

# Summing Up

This chapter presented seven steps for creating change. They are:

- **Step 1. Mobilize energy and commitment through joint identification of business problems and their solutions.** Remember: You can't order energy and commitment the way you would a monthly report; but you can generate energy and commitment if you involve people in the process.

- **Step 2. Develop a shared vision of how to organize and manage for competitiveness.** The last thing you want are several competing visions of what should be done. And once you have the vision, be sure that people see it as in their personal best interest.

- **Step 3. Identify the leadership.** You need the best people involved, and you need them at all levels. Look to the managers of change-targeted units for that leadership. *Do not* put leadership in the hands of staff personnel.

- **Step 4. Focus on results, not on activities.** Don't get wrapped up in "sound good, look good, feel good" activities. Concentrate on things that will contribute directly and tangibly to bottom-line improvement.

- **Step 5. Start change at the periphery, then let it spread to other units without pushing it from the top.** You are much more likely to change the entire organization by encouraging change in peripheral units, and letting that change spread.

- **Step 6. Institutionalize success through formal policies, systems, and structures.** And don't forget to implement ways to measure the change!

- **Step 7. Monitor and adjust strategies in response to problems in the change process.** Remember that some people will quit, some elements of your change agenda will fail, and competitors may change their tactics. So be flexible.

Also covered in this chapter was a list of typical mistakes to avoid:

- imposing a canned solution;

- driving change from the top;

- putting HR in charge;

- banking on a technical solution; and

- trying to change everything at once.

If you implement each of the seven steps effectively, and are able to avoid the common mistakes, your change goals are likely to be met.

# Social and Human Factors

*Reactions to Change*

## Key Topics Covered in This Chapter

- *The rank and file, and how they respond to change*

- *Change resisters, and how to deal with them*

- *Change agents—the people who can make things happen*

ORGANIZATIONS are inherently social systems. The people in these systems have identities, relationships, communities, attitudes, emotions, and differentiated powers. So when you try to change any part of the system, all of these factors come into play, adding many layers of complexity to a change process. Successful management of change requires that you recognize the primacy of people factors and the social systems in which they operate.

The rank and file, the resisters, and the change agents are the three sets of players typically encountered in a change initiative. Each has unique characteristics, and each requires a different style of management.

## The Rank and File

If you've spent much time observing life in the forest, you've probably noticed how animals establish routines. Deer, for example, create paths between their daytime sleeping areas and the streams, fields, and meadows where they look for food and water after dark. They stick to those paths as long as they are safe and offer few impediments to movement.

People also develop routines. Think about your own routine on a typical Saturday morning. Sleep until 8. Start a load of laundry. Cook the nice breakfast you never have time to make during the week. Pay the week's bills. Take the dog for a walk to the park. Chances are that you have routines at work as well. Like the woodland deer, people follow trails that are familiar, comfortable, safe, and satisfying. And they aren't eager to change unless given compelling reasons to do so. People also have "social routines" at work—associations with coworkers that satisfy their needs as social animals—and changes that impinge on those routines are equally unwelcome.

Occasional diversions from routines and existing social patterns add variety and interest—which please us. But diversions may also create tension, anxiety, discomfort, and even fear. As the late long-shoreman-philosopher Eric Hoffer wrote in *The Ordeal of Change:* "It is my impression that no one really likes the new. We are afraid of it." He notes that even small changes from the routine can be upsetting.

> *Back in 1936 I spent a good part of the year picking peas. I started out early in January in the Imperial Valley [of California] and drifted north-ward, picking peas as they ripened, until I picked the last peas of the season in June, around Tracy. Then I shifted all the way to Lake County, where for the first time I was going to pick string beans. And I still re-member how hesitant I was that first morning as I was about to address myself to the string bean vines. Would I be able to pick string beans? Even the change from peas to string beans had in it elements of fear.*
>
> *In the case of drastic change the uneasiness is of course deeper and more lasting. We can never be really prepared for that which is wholly new. We have to adjust ourselves and every radical adjustment is a crisis in self-esteem: we undergo a test, we have to prove ourselves. It needs in-ordinate self-confidence to face drastic change without inner trembling.*[1]

Certainly no two people feel the same "trembling" described by Hoffer. And some individuals are absolutely energized by change. The Myers-Briggs personality framework addresses this broad spec-trum. At one end of the spectrum, for example, it describes a person who likes a planned and organized approach to life (a "judging" per-son). He or she likes things settled. At the other end of the spectrum is the "perceiving" person who prefers open options and a flexible and spontaneous approach to life.[2] You probably have people repre-senting both types in your organization, and as a manager, you need to learn to deal with the full range of personalities. In particular:

- Think about the people who will participate in your change initiative. Who will react negatively to having their routines disrupted, and who will positively enjoy the experience? Make a list.

- Once you've identified people likely to be uncomfortable with change, think about their roles in the change initiative. They probably aren't the ones you'll want in key positions where initiative and enthusiasm are needed. Think, too, about how these individuals can be helped through the process.

- For individuals with pro-change dispositions, consider ways to optimize the energy they bring to the program, and how they can work with others.

And don't forget about yourself. Like everyone else you have a unique disposition to change. You either love it, hate it, or (more likely) you're somewhere between those extremes.

Discovery Learning, Inc. of Greensboro, North Carolina, has developed a helpful methodology for measuring an individual's disposition to change, indicating where that person is likely to fall on a "preferred style" continuum.[3] In their model, "Conservers" occupy one end of the continuum. Conservers are people who prefer current circumstances over the unknown—people who are more comfortable with gradual change than with anything radical. Occupying the opposite end of the spectrum are the "Originators," who prefer more rapid and radical change. "Originators are representative of the reengineering approach to change," according to Discovery Learning. "The goal of an Originator is to challenge existing structure, resulting in fast, fundamentally different, even systemic changes."[4] Occupying a middle position between these two extremes are the "Pragmatists" who support change when it clearly addresses current challenges. Pragmatists are less wedded to the existing structure than to structures that are likely to be successful. (See "Change Style Characteristics" for more on how Discovery Learning generalizes the characteristics of people who represent these three change style preferences.)

## Change Style Characteristics

### When Facing Change, Conservers:

- Generally appear deliberate, disciplined, and organized

- Prefer change that maintains current structure

- May operate from conventional assumptions

- Enjoy predictability

- May appear cautious and inflexible

- May focus on details and the routine

- Honor tradition and established practice

### When Facing Change, Pragmatists:

- May appear practical, agreeable, flexible

- Prefer change that emphasizes workable outcomes

- Are more focused on results than structure

- Operate as mediators and catalysts for understanding

- Are open to both sides of an argument

- May take more of a middle-of-the-road approach

- Appear more team-oriented

### When Facing Change, Originators:

- May appear unorganized, undisciplined, unconventional, and spontaneous

- Prefer change that challenges current structure

*Continued*

- Will likely challenge accepted assumptions

- Enjoy risk and uncertainty

- May be impractical and miss important details

- May appear as visionary and systemic in their thinking

- Can treat accepted policies and procedures with little regard

SOURCE: W. Christopher Musselwhite and Robyn Ingram, *Change Style Indicator®* (Greensboro, NC: Copyright © 2000, Discovery Learning Inc.), 5–7. Used with permission.

Knowing where your coworkers stand—and where you stand— in a change preference continuum such as this one can help you be more effective in managing the people side of a change initiative.

## The Resisters

"The reformer has enemies in all those who profit by the old order," Machiavelli warned his readers. And what held true in sixteenth-century Italy remains true today. Some people clearly enjoy advantages that—rightly or wrongly—they view as threatened by change. They may perceive change as endangering their livelihoods, their perks, their workplace social arrangements, or their status in the organization. Others know that their specialized skills will be rendered less valuable. For example, when a supplier of automotive hydraulic steering systems switched in the late 1990s to electronic steering technology, employees with expertise in hoses, valves, and fluid pressure were suddenly less important. The know-how they had developed over long careers was suddenly less valuable for the company.

Any time people perceive themselves as losers in a change initiative, expect resistance. Resistance may be passive, in the form of non-commitment to the goals and the process for reaching them, or active, in the form of direct opposition or subversion. How will you deal with that resistance?

Change masters have dealt with resisters in different ways over the years. French revolutionaries used the guillotine. The Bolsheviks had resisters shot or packed off to the gulags. Mao and his communist followers sent them to "reeducation" camps. Employment laws have removed these proven techniques from the corporate change master's tool kit, but there are other things you can do. You can begin by identifying potential resisters and try to redirect them. Here's where you can start:

- Always try to answer the question, "Where and how will change create pain or loss in the organization?"

- Identify people who have something to lose, and try to anticipate how they will respond.

- Communicate the "why" of change to potential resisters. Explain the urgency of moving away from established routines or arrangements.

- Emphasize the benefits of change to potential resisters. Those benefits might be greater future job security, higher pay, and so forth. There's no guarantee that the benefits of change will exceed the losses for these individuals. However, explaining the benefits will help shift their focus from negatives to positives.

- Help resisters find new roles—roles that represent genuine contributions *and* mitigate their losses.

- Remember that many people resist change because it represents a loss of control over their daily lives. You can return some of that control by making them active partners in the change program.

If these interventions fail, move resisters out of your unit. You cannot afford to let a few disgruntled individuals subvert the progress of the entire group. But don't make them "walk the plank." Do what you can to relocate them to positions where their particular skills can be better used. That's what the innovator of electronic steering systems did. That company still had plenty of business supplying hydraulic systems to car and truck manufacturers, so it employed its hydraulic specialists in those units even as it hired electronic engineers for its expanding new business.

As you consider resisters, don't forget that your own approach to initiating or managing change may be contributing to the problem. We noted in the previous chapter that "technical" solutions imposed from the outside often breed resistance because they fail to recognize the social dimension of work. Paul Lawrence made this point many years ago in his classic *Harvard Business Review* article "How to Deal With Resistance to Change."[5] In looking at interrelationships among employees Lawrence found that change originating among employees who work closely together is usually implemented smoothly. But change imposed by outsiders threatens powerful social bonds, generating resentment and resistance. So be sure to evaluate what part you may be playing in the resistance problem.

### Dealing with Passive Resisters

Earlier, we described passive resistance to change as noncommitment to goals and the process for reaching them. Passive resisters frustrate managers. While they don't sabotage the program, they certainly don't help the initiative move forward.

The reason that a person won't change, explain psychologists Robert Kegan and Lisa Laskow Lahey, is that he or she has a "competing commitment"—a subconscious, hidden goal that conflicts with the *stated* commitment.[6] For example, a project leader who is dragging his feet may have an unrecognized competing commitment to avoid tougher assignments that may come his way if he's too successful with the current project. A supervisor who cannot seem to get on board with the new team-based approach to problem-solving may be worried that she will be seen as incompetent if she cannot solve problems herself.

Though competing commitments are likely to be lodged deep in an employee's psyche, some serious probing on your part can sometimes get them to the surface, where you and the employee can deal with them. The most practical advice here is to engage in one-on-one communication with the passive resister. You need to find out what's keeping this person from participating in an active way.

## The Change Agents

Think for a moment about the big, big changes in the world over the centuries. Chances are that you can associate individuals with each of those changes. Copernicus and Galileo ultimately changed our view of where we stand relative to our neighbors in the solar system. Martin Luther split Christendom in two and contributed indirectly to the rise of nation states in Europe. Charles Darwin's theory on natural selection torpedoed the accepted wisdom on humankind's history. Karl Marx, a thinker, and Vladimir Lenin, a doer, created a communist movement that, at its apex, held sway over almost half the world. Henry Ford and his engineers developed a new approach to manufacturing—the assembly line—that fundamentally altered the auto industry and many other industries. In each of these cases, someone who thought differently had a major impact on human history. None began with serious resources or backing, all were outsiders, and all faced substantial opposition. All were what we call *change agents*.

Change agents are catalysts who get the ball rolling, even if they do not necessarily do most of the pushing. Everett Rogers described them as figures with one foot in the old world and one in the new—creators of a bridge across which others can travel.[7] They help others to see what the problems are, and convince them to grapple with them. Change agents, in his view, fulfill critical roles. They:

- articulate the need for change;

- are accepted by others as trustworthy and competent (people must accept the messenger before they accept the message);

- see and diagnose problems from the perspective of their audience;

- motivate people to change;

- work through others in translating intent into action;

- stabilize the adoption of innovation; and

- foster self-renewing behavior in others so that they can "go out of business" as change agents.

Who in your organization has these characteristics? Are you one of them? It is important to identify the change agents so that you can place them in key positions during a change effort. In a self-regenerating company, you'll find change agents in many different operating units and at all different levels. (See "Tips for Identifying Change Agents" for more information.)

Can change agents be created? Perhaps. One German electronics firm did so in the 1990s when it faced poor financial performance, sagging morale, and weak competitiveness. The company was over-consulted and under-managed. Many of its best young employees were unhappy with consecutive years of losses and dimming prospects. The company's rigid corporate hierarchy was partly to blame. Management recognized that it had to distribute authority and decision making more broadly. To accomplish this it created a change agent program that sent two dozen hand-picked employees to the United States for special training, which included abundant exposure to entrepreneurial American firms. Once the training program was completed, the newly minted change agents were transferred back to their units, where they worked to break the mold of the old hierarchical system.

General Motors attempted something very similar in its joint venture with Toyota: the NUMMI small car assembly plant in California. That plant was run according to Toyota's world-beating production methods, and GM rotated manufacturing managers through the plant to learn Toyota's methods and, hopefully, bring a working knowledge of those methods back to Detroit. As described earlier, furniture maker Herman Miller sought the same result when it moved managers from its SQA unit into its traditional operating units; it figured that these individuals would infect others with their faster, more accurate approach to manufacturing and fulfillment.

Your search for change agents shouldn't necessarily be limited to company personnel. Every so often it's wise to look outside for people who have the skills and attitudes required to stir things up and get the organization moving in a new and more promising direction. This approach is not without risk, since the outsider's lack of familiarity with the company's culture may result in unforeseen turmoil. For a discussion of this issue, see "The Insider-Outsider as Change Agent" and its *Harvard Business Review* excerpt.

## Tips for Identifying Change Agents

- Find out who people listen to. Change agents lead with the power of their ideas. But be warned: These may not be employees with formal authority to lead.

- Be alert to people who "think otherwise." Change agents are not satisfied with things as they are—a fact that may not endear them to management.

- Take a close look at new employees who have come from outside the circle of traditional competitors. They may not be infected with the same mind-set as everyone else.

- Look for people with unusual training or experience. For example, if all your marketing people have business degrees and heavy quantitative research backgrounds, look for the oddball liberal arts major who has a degree in social anthropology. Chances are she sees the world through a different lens.

## The Insider-Outsider as Change Agent

Many companies feel that the only way to create change and make it stick is to bring in outsiders with no ties to the status quo. Others fear that outsiders who don't understand the business, its culture, and its values will simply create disruption. Writing in the *Harvard Business Review*, Donald Sull recommends that leadership for change be invested in individuals who represent both sides of the coin: a fresh perspective on the business *and* a solid appreciation for the company's culture.

*Guiding a company through big changes requires a difficult balancing act. The company's heritage has to be respected even as it's being resisted. It's often assumed that outsider managers are best suited to lead such an effort since they're not bound by the company's historical*

*Continued*

*formula. . . . Typically, outsiders are so quick to throw out all the old ways of working that they end up doing more harm than good.*

*The approach I recommend is to look for new leaders from within the company but from outside the core business. These managers, whom I call inside-outsiders, can be drawn from the company's smaller divisions, from international operations, or from staff functions. . . .*

*Insider-outsiders have led many of the most dramatic corporate transformations in recent times. Jack Welch spent most of his career in GE's plastics business; Jürgen Schrempp was posted in South Africa before returning to run [DaimlerChrysler]; and Domenico De Sole served as the Gucci Group's legal counsel before leading that company's dramatic rejuvenation.*

*Another alternative is to assemble management teams that leverage the strengths of both insiders and outsiders. When [Lou] Gerstner took over at IBM, he didn't force out all the old guard. Most operating positions continued to be staffed by IBM veterans with decades of experience, but they were supported by outsiders in key staff slots and marketing roles. The combination of perspectives has allowed IBM to use old strengths to fuel its passage down an entirely new course.*

*Finally, inside managers can break free of their old formulas by imagining themselves as outsiders, as Intel's executives did in deciding to abandon the memory business. Intel had pioneered the market for memory chips, and for most of its executives, employees, and customers, Intel meant memory. As new competitors entered the market, however, Intel saw its share of the memory business dwindle. . . .*

*Although Intel had built an attractive microprocessor business during this time, it clung to the memory business until its chairman, Gordon Moore, and its president, Andy Grove, sat down and deliberately imagined what would happen if they were replaced with outsiders. They agreed that outsiders would get out of the memory business—and that's exactly what Moore and Grove did. While a company's competitive formula exerts a tremendous gravitational pull, thinking like outsiders can help insiders to break free.*[a]

[a] Donald N. Sull, "Why Good Companies Go Bad," *Harvard Business Review* 77, no. 4 (July–August 1999): 50.

# Summing Up

Change is complicated by the fact that organizations are social systems whose participants have identities, relationships, communities, routines, emotions, and differentiated powers. Thus managers must be alert to how a change will conflict with existing social systems and individual routines.

This chapter explored the three identity categories that employees typically fall into:

- The *rank and file* is likely to include people who exhibit a spectrum of reactions to change. This chapter adopted the terms "conservers," "pragmatists," and "originators" to describe how different people respond to change. Knowing where your coworkers stand—and where you stand—in a change preference continuum such as this one can help you be more effective in managing the people side of a change initiative.

- *Change resisters* will either drag their feet or actively attempt to undermine your efforts. You can identify potential resisters by determining where and how change will create pain or loss in the organization. Once you've identified them, there are several things you can do to neutralize their resistance or make them active participants. These include: explaining the urgent need to change, describing how change will produce benefits for them, and finding new ways in which they can contribute. People who do not respond to these efforts should be moved out of your unit.

- *Change agents* see the need for change and articulate it effectively to others. They are critical catalysts for a change initiative and should be placed in key positions. This chapter has provided tips for identifying change agents.

# Containment

*Preventing a Bad Situation
from Becoming Worse*

## Key Topics Covered in This Chapter

- *Rule 1: Use quick and decisive action*

- *Rule 2: Put people first*

- *Rule 3: Be physically at the scene*

- *Rule 4: Communicate liberally*

L EFT UNCHECKED, some crises will move from bad to worse. This is what happened during the pedophile scandal that rocked the Catholic diocese of Boston over a period of years. The more Church officials dithered and denied, the worse the situation became. A crisis in one area can also create crisis elsewhere if not checked promptly. For example, if embezzlement by a prominent executive is discovered, the media plays up the story. While management is occupied with the legal issues of the embezzlement, other bad things happen. Because of the damage done to the company's reputation, talented executives may be pirated by competitors, promising employee candidates are likely to take jobs elsewhere, and the company's sales reps will report that some key customers have shifted their orders to other suppliers. Meanwhile, outraged shareholders may even bring a lawsuit against board members, citing their failure to fulfill their fiduciary responsibilities.

This chapter offers four rules for containing a crisis once it is recognized. *Crisis containment* is defined here as the decisions and actions that aim to keep a crisis from growing worse.

Crisis containment has a lot in common with the work of emergency medical technicians (EMTs)—namely, to stabilize the situation until more decisive action can be mounted, as in the following example:

*An EMT van has just arrived at the scene of a traffic accident. The driver of one of the vehicles is breathing and semiconscious but already in shock. He is also bleeding heavily from a laceration to his arm. There are no other visible signs of injury.*

*The EMTs know at a glance that this driver is in grave danger from blood loss, from shock, and from any internal injuries that they are not equipped to detect or treat. Their job is clear: to keep the crash victim's condition from worsening while they rush him to the hospital. Once there, doctors and nurses will take the steps necessary to restore this driver to health. So the EMTs load the victim into the van, and one drives while the other applies a pressure bandage to the arm wound and takes steps to prevent the patient from going into shock.*

The EMTs in that example are practicing crisis containment. When crisis strikes your company, think like an EMT. Identify the problem, and then figure out what you can do to stabilize the situation and prevent the crisis from growing worse. This stop-gap action will give your crisis team time to implement an appropriate contingency plan.

## Rule 1: Act Quickly and Decisively

Above all, observe the first rule of crisis containment, which is to act quickly and decisively. This is what Johnson & Johnson (J&J) officials did back in 1982 when the first ties between customer illness and fatalities were associated with Tylenol, the company's market-dominating, nonprescription painkiller. Within a three-day period, seven people died after using Tylenol—all victims of a pharma-terrorist who planted cyanide-laced capsules in bottles of the product. How many tampered bottles were out there? Would more die? Would copycat felons strike elsewhere in the country? Company officials had no way to answer those questions, so they acted decisively, withdrawing all Tylenol products from drugstore shelves—all 22 million bottles. And they kept the product off store shelves until they had developed a tamper-proof container in which they and the public had confidence. This action cost J&J hundreds of million of dollars in the short term but contained the crisis and made it possible for the brand to regain its stature and profitability in the long term. That swift action prevented a criminal act from further undermining public confidence in Johnson & Johnson's global enterprise and its many products.

The Johnson & Johnson case underscores the importance of acting quickly and decisively in crisis situations. This is more easily said than done. Good managers know that quality decisions depend on having a solid base of information and sound analysis of the situation. But both are usually absent in a crisis. Information is limited, and you don't have time to gather as much as you need. And whatever action you take is likely to be costly and expose your intervention to lots of second-guessing once the crisis has passed.

Limited information in most cases should not prevent a rapid response, particularly if the contingency planning recommended earlier has been done. For example, if someone smells smoke in our building, we don't have to know the extent of the fire or where it is located in order to act. We act immediately to evacuate the building and call the fire department. If we've practiced contingency planning, the fire department's phone number will be on our speed-dial, and every employee will have been trained in rapid evacuation of the building. Should we worry about a false alarm? No. We should know in advance that most building evacuations are based on false alarms. But the cost of a false alarm is nothing compared to the cost of multiple deaths and the property damage caused by a fire that may occur if evacuation is delayed.

## Rule 2: Put People First

The Johnson & Johnson Tylenol case and the example of a fire emergency illustrate the second rule of crisis containment: Make people your first concern. In the end, material things can be replaced—and most are already insured against loss—as in this case:

> *A torrential rainstorm caused serious water damage to a section of an office building, destroying electronic equipment, carpeting, paper records, and the work space used by ten employees on the ground floor. Robert, the office manager, was on the scene the next morning as employees showed up for work. He helped those employees and a hired crew clean up the area and dry it out. Within twenty-four hours the place was ready for business once again.*

*Three days later, several employees complained of breathing prob-*
*lems and headaches. Many suspected that the carpeting was to blame.*
*Though it had been thoroughly cleaned and dried after the flood, many*
*believed that the carpet was infested with mold. The manager thought*
*about his options. He could have the carpet cleaned again and hope*
*that the problem would go away. He could put in a request to have the*
*carpet replaced, but that would involve waiting several days for budget*
*approval and still more for installation. Instead, Robert ordered all car-*
*peting in the area to be removed and replaced. "I'll worry about the cost*
*later," he told himself.*

Robert's approach in that case satisfied the first and second rules
of crisis containment: He acted quickly and decisively, and he put
people above material goods. By replacing the suspicious carpeting
immediately he demonstrated that the health of employees was
more important than any other consideration. Someone might later
complain that the cost was not in the budget, but crisis costs are *never*
in the budget. So within the bounds of good sense, don't worry
about the budget or the other workplace procedures that govern
how things are done under normal conditions. Instead, do what it
takes to keep people safe.

## Rule 3: Be on the Scene

The third rule of crisis containment is for top people to be physically on the scene as quickly as possible. A physical presence sends a
loud and clear message that those people think the situation is ex-
tremely important. Their absence sends the opposite message, that
they have other priorities at the moment. Think of the impact of this
message on people affected by the crisis. As author and practitioner
Laurence Barton bluntly put it, "People want to see their leaders in a
crisis."[1] Here's what can happen when the people in charge choose
to avoid the spotlight:

*The sinking of the nuclear submarine* Kursk *in August 2000 was a*
*major blow to the reputation and morale of the Russian Navy. To make*

*matters worse, senior officials failed to mount a rescue mission and later had to call on Western rivals to recover the ship. Still worse, 118 crew members were lost.*

*The Russian government's handling of the crisis was equally ineffective. The Ministry of Defense initially downplayed the seriousness of the incident, saying that the sub had merely run aground during a training exercise. The crew, it told the public, was in no immediate danger. Later, as details began to leak out, the ministry spread rumors of a collision with a NATO submarine. These pronouncements were proved false as more information became available, indicating that the government was more interested in covering up the debacle than in resolving it and saving the crew.*

*The sinking of the Kursk was also an enormous public relations blunder for President Vladimir Putin. Putin, who was vacationing at a southern Russia resort at the time, appeared in casual clothes to tell the television audience that the situation was under control. He then disappeared for several days. His failure to take a personal hand in managing the crisis angered the public and outraged families of the ill-fated crew. As reported by the Los Angeles Times, "Putin seemed aloof and distant after the Kursk sank. He stayed on vacation for nearly a week at the Black Sea resort of Sochi and didn't request foreign rescuers until August 16. Instead of going to the submarine's Arctic port to energize rescue efforts, he portrayed himself last week as a functionary who didn't want to get in the way."[2] Eventually, the Russian leader found time to visit the Kursk's home base, where he was greeted by a hostile and angry crowd.*

You can almost forgive Vladimir Putin for failing to observe Rule 3 of crisis containment. After all, his background as a KGB official had not prepared him for handling anything like this. The term *public relations* probably wasn't even in the secretive KGB's vocabulary. It's less easy to forgive Western executives for making this mistake. But they break this rule just the same. One example was Exxon's CEO Lawrence Rawls, who didn't appear at the site of the disastrous *Exxon Valdez* accident for three weeks after the event had taken place.[3] Instead of sending its top person to the scene of history's biggest and most damaging oil spill, Exxon sent a district functionary. The example set by New York City Mayor Rudy Giuliani stands in sharp contrast to Russia's Putin and Exxon's Rawls. Giuliani seemed omnipresent in the aftermath of the 9/11 disaster. He was on the scene within minutes of the terrorist strikes against the Twin Towers, in command, available to the press, and present at dozen of funerals in the weeks that followed.

This is not to say that a CEO must take command of every crisis. For example, the head of a huge retail chain such as Home Depot should not feel compelled to rush to the scene of a store fire. That would be nice, but not strictly necessary. The local or district manager could fill the same role. The response should be proportional to the crisis. On the other hand, if the store fire killed customers or employees, the crisis level would demand the presence of the CEO.

## Rule 4: Communicate Liberally

Fires, power outages, hostile takeovers, major product failures, and other damaging events create a sudden and substantial demand for information. People want to know what happened, how it happened, what will happen next, and how they should respond. Rule 4 of crisis containment requires that those questions be answered to the extent that answers are available.

Every contingency plan and every crisis management team should have a communication plan at the ready to provide information as it become available. Obviously, that plan cannot have a stock set of answers for people's questions, but it can and should have all the mechanisms for communicating in place. These include:

- A blueprint for gathering available facts

- A designated spokesperson

- The names and phone numbers of the people and institutions that should be contacted in the wake of a crisis (managers, supervisors, fire and police, the media, and so forth)

- An information hot line that people can call for information and instructions

- A single group e-mail address that can send a message to all employees and directors at once

- An off-site communications center equipped with phones, cell phones, and Internet connections (being off-site is important in the case of a building fire; cell phones are important because landlines might not be working)

Do you have a communication plan in place? Would it meet the requirements of a serious crisis?

### Counter Rumors and Speculation with Facts

A sudden crisis creates an information vacuum. Something has happened, but no one knows what—at least initially. People are hungry for information. Just as nature abhors a vacuum, empty information space tends to fill itself with whatever comes along, even if it is nothing more than speculation and rumor. If you have any doubts about this, turn on your television or radio the next time there is a major catastrophe, the outbreak of war, or a political scandal. Broadcasters go into full-time coverage mode for such events and bring in all their talking heads to fill airtime. In the early stages, most discourse is pure speculation, since broadcasters will say just about anything to fill dead airtime. During the first day of the Clinton-Lewinsky scandal, for example, a fact-deprived political reporter for National Public Radio struggled desperately for something to say about the salacious scandal's impact on Clinton's political future. "People are saying . . . ," she intoned, indicating that even the legitimate media had plunged deep into the rumor barrel.

The fourth rule of crisis containment is to communicate the facts that exist—no more, no less. Doing so will help fill the information vacuum, leaving less space for rumor and speculation. A good communicator can also dampen rumors directly as in these examples:

*A number of employees are concerned that our proposed merger with Oscar's Cat Food, Inc. will result in closure of our Nashville regional plant. This concern is unfounded. I can tell you that there are no plans to close the Nashville plant.*

*As many have speculated, the fire of October 27 caused considerable damage to our information systems equipment. The full extent of that damage is currently being accessed. In the meantime, our off-site backup system is fully operational and capable of handling all of our information and transaction requirements during the recovery period. Beginning tomorrow, all orders will be channeled through our Limerick, Ireland, customer service center, processed by the off-site data center, and filled by our regional distribution facilities.*

*Several recent news stories have reported alleged improprieties in the management of your company's employee pension plan. At this point, none of the allegations have been substantiated. The board of directors has engaged an independent audit firm, Farnsworth & Farrell, to conduct a thorough investigation, which is now in its early stages. A full report is anticipated in early November of this year and will be made available to all. Any interim findings will be communicated to you without delay.*

As you communicate, get out all the bad news at once. It is better and more honest to do this than to release a continuing stream of bad news. Putting out all the bad news at once is similar to quickly pulling off a bandage. It hurts for a moment, but then the hurt goes away. Likewise, once all the bad news is out, subsequent communications are likely to be dominated by good news. For example:

*We are please to report that a review of fire damage at our data center by IT Vice President Jane Harley and COO Jake Newhall found that losses are much less serious than anticipated, and that the system will be up and running sooner than earlier believed. Meanwhile, the off-site backup system is in its second day of processing customer orders and is doing so without a hitch!*

## Speak with One Voice

Even though your crisis management team may have chosen a spokesperson to communicate with the media, the media is likely to seek out others for their stories and opinions. For example, if a senior manager has just been slapped with a sexual harassment lawsuit, female employees are likely to get phone calls at work and at home from reporters seeking a good story. These employees may or may not be in command of the facts. And what they say could make matters worse. So encourage employees to refer all inquiries to the company spokesperson.

### Communicate with Stakeholders and the Public

In containing a crisis, employees are a natural first concern. But do not forget about other stakeholders: shareholders, suppliers, customers, and strategic business partners, among others. They will want to know what's going on and what to expect. The same goes for the public in the geographic areas where your company operates. Give the public the same facts that you give to your employees and stakeholders; a press release is often the quickest and best approach.

Remember too that what you say and how you say it are both critical. The way you communicate may precipitate actions that can make the crises worse—or better. A crisis, by definition, means that there is bad news. Dealing with pain and anger early can forestall far worse problems later on. Your goal is to contain the overall crisis, not to make the present moment easier.

### When in Doubt, Let Your Training, Values, and Instincts Guide You

Crisis containment can strain a person's capacity to make good decisions. Facts are few, and decision makers must act swiftly or risk a still greater crisis situation. There is no time to gather more information,

calmly consider alternative responses, or think about the unanticipated consequences of each response. Think for a moment of what it
must be like to be a 23-year-old lieutenant whose infantry platoon
has just walked into an ambush. Two men are already hit, and everyone else is pinned down by withering fire from two directions—or
is it three? The heavy undergrowth makes it impossible to see what
you're up against. The noise is deafening and everyone's scared, including you. You know that if you stay put, enemy mortars will have
time to zero in. If you move, your men will be exposed. The platoon
sergeant crawls to within shouting distance: "What are we gonna do,
sir?" Yes, what are you going to do?

If you are charged with containing a dangerous crisis, you and
the young lieutenant have much in common. Little information is
available, and the situation is desperate. But you cannot allow indeci-
sion to paralyze you; you must act and act quickly, before the situation becomes worse. If the right thing to do isn't apparent, do this:

- **Fall back on your planning and training.** If you've done contingency planning, you will already have thought through how
  best to respond to a range of potential problems. And if you
  tested your plans with simulations and training exercises, you'll
  have a set of viable options for immediate action.

## Seek Out Wise Counsel

If you must make an important decision quickly and with insufficient information, don't feel that you must do it alone; seek
the counsel of people you trust. Ideally, your crisis management
team includes trustworthy people who think clearly in difficult
situations. Perhaps simulations have prepared you to work together under stressful conditions. If you don't have such a team,
keep in touch with a wise and trusted friend or mentor—a person you can rely on to objectively critique your ideas and provide good advice. Test your ideas with those counselors. They
have experienced similar situations. They may suggest alternative courses of action that you have failed to consider.

- **Let your values guide you.** Your ethical sense of right and wrong is a powerful compass. If the landscape is murky, take your direction from your values.

- **Listen to your instincts.** If something feels wrong, it probably *is* wrong. Don't do it.

## Summing Up

- Observe the four rules of crisis containment:

  1. **Act quickly and decisively.** Delay will only allow the situation to grow worse.

  2. **Put people first.** Building, inventory, credit rates, and corporate reputations can all be recouped; the lives of customers and employees cannot.

  3. **Get top people to the crisis scene as quickly as possible.** This will demonstrate that the crisis is being taken seriously.

  4. **Communicate liberally.** This is the best way to counter rumors and speculation.

- When the right course of action is not clear, let your training, your values, and your instincts guide you.

# 5

# Implementation

*Putting Your Plan in Motion*

## Key Topics Covered in This Chapter

* *How to enlist the support and involvement of key people in a change initiative*

* *Tips for crafting a good implementation plan*

* *The importance of supporting the plan with consistent behaviors*

* *How to develop enabling structures (i.e., training, pilot programs, and a reward system)*

* *Ways to celebrate milestones*

* *The importance of relentless communication*

* *The role of consultants*

O NCE people are convinced that change is necessary, and that the change vision is the right one, it's time to move forward with implementation.

Implementation rarely proceeds smoothly. Once people get into the nitty-gritty of implementing their change initiative, they discover that there is no tidy, step-by-step march to the envisioned future. Mistakes are made. External factors upset schedules. Key people quit or are transferred. Different groups forget to communicate with each other.

A survey conducted in the mid-1980s identified seven implementation problems that occurred in at least 60 percent of the ninety-three firms polled:[1]

1. Implementation took more time than originally allocated (76 percent).

2. Major problems surfaced during implementation that had not been identified beforehand (74 percent).

3. Coordination of implementation activities (for example, task forces or committees) was not effective enough (66 percent).

4. Competing activities and crises distracted attention from implementing this strategic decision (64 percent).

5. Capabilities (skill and abilities) of employees involved with the implementation were not sufficient (63 percent).

6. Training and instruction given to lower-level employees were not adequate (62 percent).

7. Uncontrollable factors in the external environment had an adverse impact on implementation (60 percent).

Other implementation problems include insufficient support for change or unclear goals. Although implementation can be a tricky and unpredictable challenge, you can improve the odds of success if you enlist the support and involvement of key people, craft a solid plan, support the plan with consistent behaviors, develop enabling structures, celebrate milestone successes, and communicate relentlessly.

## Enlist the Support and Involvement of Key People

Your implementation will go more smoothly if it has the backing and involvement of key people—and not just the CEO and his or her court. It is also critical to enlist managers and employees whom others respect, individuals with key technical skills, people with access to vital resources, and the informal leaders to whom people naturally turn for direction and advice.

So how can you pinpoint these people? Authors Michael Tushman and Charles O'Reilly offer this advice:

> To determine who these key individuals are and what their responses to the change might be, ask: Who has the power to make or break the change? Who controls critical resources or expertise? Then think through how the change will likely affect each of these individuals and how each is likely to react toward the change. Who will gain or lose something. . . . Are there blocs of individuals likely to mobilize against or in support of the change effort?[2]

Enlisting support entails building an effective team of change makers that can act together toward stated goals. But how can you be sure you've picked the right people for the team? Here's a set of questions that will help you know if your team has the right stuff:[3]

- Are enough of your company's key players (people in relevant positions of power) members of the team?

- Do members of the team have the relevant *expertise* to do the job and make intelligent decisions?

- Does the team include the needed *range* of perspectives and disciplines to do the job and make intelligent decisions?

- Does the team include people with sufficient credibility so that employees and management will treat its decisions seriously?

- Does the team include people with demonstrated leadership skills?

- Are the team members capable of forgoing their personal immediate interests in favor of the larger organizational goal?

If you answered "yes" to most of these questions, the team guiding the change effort is strong and in a good position to succeed. If you said "no" to any questions, it might be a good idea to revisit your team choices. (For more on selecting team members, see "Tips on Who Should *Not* Be on the Team.")

## Craft an Implementation Plan

While a vision may guide and inspire team members during the change process, an organization also needs a nuts-and-bolts plan for what to do, and when and how to do it. This plan should map out the effort, specifying everything from where the first meetings should be held, to the date by which the company should reasonably expect to achieve its change goals. Here are some characteristics of a good implementation plan:[4]

- **It's simple.** An overly complex plan may confuse and frustrate participants in the change effort. So if your flowchart of activities and milestones looks like the wiring diagram for the space shuttle, rethink it with an eye toward simplicity and coherence.

- **It's created by people at all affected levels.** This goes back to Step 1 of the change process, which advocates "joint identification of business problems and their solutions." The implementation

## Tips on Who Should Not Be on the Team

In his book on *Leading Change,* John Kotter recommends that you keep three types of people off your team:[a]

1. **People with big egos.** Big egos, per Kotter, fill the room, leaving little or no space for anybody else to participate or contribute. People with big egos don't always understand their own limitations and how those limitations can be complemented by the strength of others.

2. **Snakes.** Kotter describes a "snake" as the kind of person who secretly poisons relationships between team members. "A snake is an expert at telling Sally something about Fred and Fred something about Sally that undermines Sally and Fred's relationship."

3. **Reluctant players.** These are people who lack either the time or enthusiasm to provide energy to the team. Be wary of including these people on your team. Keeping them off may be difficult, however, since some reluctant players may have the expertise and/or organizational power you need.

[a] John P. Kotter, *Leading Change* (Boston, MA: Harvard Business School Press, 1996), 59–61.

plan is part of the solution, and shouldn't be imposed on the people asked to push it forward. If the implementers and other people affected by the change are involved in making the plan, they'll be more enthusiastic in supporting the initiative. Remember, too, that a plan devised solely by strategists is less likely to reflect the realities of the business and what the organization can accomplish than a plan built on the ideas of the worker bees.

- **It's structured in achievable chunks.** Overly ambitious plans are usually doomed to failure. People look at them and say, "We'll never get this done—not in our lifetimes." They'll be defeated from the beginning. So build a plan that can be tackled in manageable, achievable segments.

- **It specifies roles and responsibilities.** Like every endeavor, a change plan should detail clear roles and responsibilities for everyone involved. Every planned outcome should be the acknowledged responsibility of one or more individuals. Those individuals should publicly state that they welcome and accept the responsibility. Input from all levels of the organization will help to achieve this role-oriented focus.

- **It's flexible.** As noted in the previous chapter, change programs seldom follow their planned trajectories or timetables. Thus, a good implementation plan is a living document open to revision. Organizations that lock themselves into rigid schedules, goals, and events, ultimately find themselves detached from the shifting world that surrounds them.

## Support the Plan with Consistent Behaviors and Messages

Once the need for change has been articulated convincingly and broad support has been enlisted, that support must be maintained through a set of consistent behaviors and messages. Inconsistency in either will send a damaging message—that management is either not serious about implementing change or unwilling to do its part.

Consider this example: Not many years ago, one of the American Big Three automakers underwent a painful restructuring. Everyone was asked to sacrifice by giving up benefits today in order to achieve greater competitiveness and prosperity tomorrow. Thousands of middle managers and employees were laid off and the company's union was asked to forego pay and benefit increases. Because the company had made a convincing case for change, people got the message and tightened their belts; even the unions pitched in. Within months, however, senior management awarded itself and other key people bonuses and substantial pay increases. Once that inconsistent behavior became public, the bonds of trust between management and the rank and file—and their unions—evaporated. Collaboration turned to open hostility that simmered for nearly ten years.

At about the same time, a company in another industry was likewise supporting a belt-tightening and restructuring program. But this one did so with highly visible and consistent deeds. Its CEO set the pace by selling the corporation's three jets and taking commercial flights on his travels—in coach class to boot. And no more limos to meet him at the airport. "I don't mind taking a cab," he told the business press. "They can get me to where I'm going just as fast." The company's other traveling executives followed the lead of their boss. People noticed.

Which of these companies do you suppose was more successful in building support for its change program?

SQA, Herman Miller's successful low-cost office furniture unit, used a consistent set of messages to support its effort to increase on-time, accurate fulfillment of orders. Everyone understood that this was the unit's key measure of successful change. So SQA managers came up with several ways to reinforce that understanding. For example, they installed signboards at every entrance to the plant, and each morning they posted the previous day's percentage of on-time orders. It was impossible to enter or leave the plant without knowing the previous day's performance. They also added the on-time order metric to internal e-mail messages. "Yesterday's percentage of on-time accurately filled orders was 99.2%." The vice president of operations even adopted the practice of randomly asking employees if they knew the previous day's score. A correct answer was rewarded with either a crisp $100 bill or a paid day off.

What messages or behaviors would be consistent with the change program at your company?

## Develop Enabling Structures

Enabling structures are the activities and programs that underpin successful implementation and are a critical part of the overall plan. Such structures include pilot programs, training, and reward systems.

Pilot programs give people opportunities to grapple with implementation and its problems on a smaller, more manageable scale. Pilots are test beds in which implementers can experiment with and de-bug change initiatives before rolling them out more broadly. These programs can be valuable proving ground since it's almost always easier and less risky to change a single department than an entire company.

Training programs can hold equal value. Motorola and General Electric developed formal training programs that served as key enablers for the ensuing quality initiatives. Xerox did the same when it set up its companywide benchmarking program in the mid-1980s. Every Xerox employee received a copy of "the little yellow book," as they called the company's how-to manual on benchmarking methods, and skilled trainers were placed in almost every operating unit of the company.

Reward systems also play an enabling role. People generally adopt behaviors that produce rewards, and abandon those that are unrewarded. Thus, if your change program asks people to either work harder, work smarter, or work in new ways, your reward system must be aligned with the desired behaviors. However, the details and pitfalls of crafting incentive programs are complex and situationally determined and thus need to be crafted within the context of each organization.

## Celebrate Milestones

Change initiatives can be long and frustrating. But you can keep up peoples' spirits and energy if you identify milestones—even small ones—and celebrate them as they are achieved. (See "Tips for Celebrating Short-Term Wins.") Celebrating a series of short-term wins can:

- neutralize skepticism about the change effort;
- provide evidence that peoples' sacrifices and hard work are paying off;
- help retain the support of senior management;
- keep up the momentum; and
- boost morale.

## Tips for Celebrating Short-Term Wins

Here are just a few ideas for celebrating short-term wins and keeping your team pumped up:

- Treat change participants to a catered lunch—and bring in an outside speaker who can talk about his or her company's success in doing something similar.

- Have a picnic.

- Take the afternoon off for a softball game.

- Recognize the deeds of exceptional contributors.

Do something grander for major successes. For example, when you've successfully reached the midpoint of the initiative, host a dinner with the CEO as guest and keynote speaker.

There is a fine line between celebrating a successful milestone and making a premature declaration of victory. Crossing it will dissipate the sense of urgency you need to keep people motivated and moving on toward future hurdles.

John Kotter, who lists "declaring victory too soon" among the reasons that transformation efforts fail, says that both change initiators and change resisters have reasons for making this mistake. "In their enthusiasm over a clear sign of progress," he writes, "the initiators go overboard. They are then joined by resistors, who are quick to spot any opportunity to stop change. . . . [T]he resistors point to the victory as a sign that the war has been won and the troops should be sent home."[5] Catastrophe follows if the weary troops accept this argument and go back to their usual activities.

So instead of declaring victory, use the credibility and momentum gained from your short-term win to muster an attack on the next milestone.

## Communicate Relentlessly

Communication is an effective tool for motivating employees, for overcoming resistance to an initiative, for preparing people for the pluses and minuses of change, and for giving employees a personal stake in the process. Effective communication can set the tone for a change program and is critical to implementation from the very start. But don't rely on a single Big Bang announcement to keep employees in line with the effort. Communication must be ongoing. (See "Putting Communication to Work" for a story emphasizing the importance of ongoing communication.) Here are eleven tips for communicating during a change effort:[6]

1. **Specify the nature of the change.** Slogans, themes, and phrases don't define what the change is expected to achieve. Communicate specific information about how the change will affect customer satisfaction, quality, market share or sales, or productivity.

2. **Explain why.** Employees are often left in the dark about the business reasons behind the change. You may have spent lots of time studying the problem and digging out the facts, but your coworkers aren't privy to that information. In addition, share with employees the various options available and why some (or one) is better than the others.

3. **Explain the scope of the change, even if it contains bad news.** Some people are more affected by change projects than others. And that leads to lots of fear-generating speculation. Fear and uncertainty can paralyze a company. You can short-circuit fear and uncertainty with the facts. But don't sugarcoat them. If people will be laid off, be up front about it. Also explain the things that will *not* change. This will help anchor people.

4. **Develop a graphic representation of the change project that people can understand and hold in their heads.** It might be a flow chart of what must happen, or a graphic image of what the changed enterprise will look like. Whatever it is, keep it clear, simple, and memorable.

5. **Predict negative aspects of implementation.** There are bound to be negatives, and people should anticipate them.

6. **Explain the criteria for success and how it will be measured.** Define success clearly, and devise metrics for progress toward it. If you fail to establish clear measures for what you aim to accomplish, how would anyone know if they had moved forward? Measure progress as you move forward—and then communicate that progress.

7. **Explain how people will be rewarded for success.** People need incentive for the added work and disruptions that change requires. Be very clear about how individuals will be rewarded for progress toward change goals.

8. **Repeat, repeat, and repeat the purpose of change and actions planned.** If the initial announcement doesn't generate questions, do not assume that employees accept the need for change—they may simply be surprised, puzzled, or shocked. So follow up your initial announcement meeting with another meeting. Follow this with communications that address individual aspects of the change project.

9. **Use a diverse set of communication styles that is appropriate for the audience.** Successful change programs build communications into their plans, using dedicated newsletters, events, e-mails, and stand-up presentations to keep people informed, involved, and keyed up. These communications should be honest about successes and failures. If people lose trust in what they are hearing, they will tune you out.

10. **Make communication a two-way proposition.** Remember, this is a shared enterprise. So, if you are a change leader, spend at least as much time listening as telling. Your attention to this point will help keep others involved and motivated. Leaders need feedback, and the hardworking implementers need opportunities to share their learning and their concerns with leaders who listen.

11. **Be a poster–boy or poster–girl for the change program.** If you are the boss, people will have their eyes on you. They will listen to your words, but will also look for inconsistencies between your words and what you communicate through body language and behavior. Do you speak and act with genuine enthusiasm? Does your tone and manner signal confidence in the project, or do you appear to be going through the motions? Try to see yourself as others see you.

## Using Consultants

We end this chapter on implementation with a brief discussion of the role of consultants, and how and when they can help you.

Consultants have been working with companies since the early

## Putting Communication to Work

Communication played a big role in the successful change program that pulled Continental Airlines out of a nosedive in the 1990s. Here's how president and CEO Greg Brenneman described Continental's approach in an article for the *Harvard Business Review:*

*When I arrived at Continental, it was a mean and lousy place to work. For years, different groups of employees had been pitted against one another in the effort to drive down labor costs. Management's implicit communication policy had been, Don't tell anybody anything unless absolutely required. As a result, most employees learned of the company's activities, plans, and performance through the press. Talk about sending a message about who matters and who doesn't.*

*On top of that, employees had no place to go with ideas or questions. There were forms for employees' suggestions on how to improve the operations, but the suggestions disappeared into a black*

*hole. Add to that the fact that corporate headquarters was locked up like Fort Knox: the president's secretary had a buzzer under her desk that she could use to summon the police.*

*Needless to say, morale was terrible. A couple of weeks after I arrived, I was walking the ramp in Houston saying hello to our mechanics and baggage handlers, and helping to throw a bag or two, when I noticed that almost all the employees had torn the Continental logos from their shirts. When I asked one mechanic why he had done this, he explained, "When I go to Wal-Mart tonight, I don't want anyone to know that I work for Continental." His response still sends chills down my spine.*

*Now, how to create a new culture is the topic of hundreds, if not thousands, of books and articles. But Gordon [Bethune] and I didn't bother with them. We agreed that a healthy culture is simply a function of several factors, namely: honesty, trust, dignity, and respect. They all go together; they reinforce one another. When they are constants in a business, people become engaged in their work. They care; they talk; they laugh. And then fun happens pretty naturally. But honesty and the rest don't just sprout up like weeds in a cornfield, especially when there has been a long drought. In a turnaround situation, people are tense and suspicious for good reason. They've been lied to. They've seen their friends get fired. They fear they will be next.*

*So cultivating honesty, trust, dignity, and respect becomes the job of the leaders. It may even be their most important job; Gordon and I certainly considered it our top priority. That's why when we took over, we started talking with employees at every opportunity. We got out there in the airports and on the planes. We loaded bags; we stood alongside the agents at ticket counters. We just talked at every opportunity about our plans for the airline and how we were going to accomplish them. In general, our communication policy changed from, Don't tell anybody anything unless absolutely required, to Tell everybody everything.*

SOURCE: Greg Brenneman, "Right Away and All at Once: How We Saved Continental," *Harvard Business Review* 76, no. 5 (September–October 1998): 176.

post-World War II era, when McKinsey and Boston Consulting Group began offering strategic planning advice to corporate executives. But the real growth in management consulting came through human resource departments when academic work in the social/behavioral sciences—particularly in psychology, sociology, social anthropology, and organizational behavior—found applications (and paying customers) in the world of business. Indeed, many in the field of management consulting see themselves as conduits through which concepts developed in the academic realm can be tested and applied in the real world.

From those HR and training origins, consultants have developed new and more lucrative practices in the field of change management. During the early 1980s, the hottest cards in the deck were total quality management and its offspring: benchmarking, *kaisan,* and service excellence. A decade later process reengineering and organizational learning were the favored corporate elixirs. More recently, consulting companies have ridden a wave of interest in enterprise—linking information systems, and helping companies design, install, and eventually manage them.

Before enlisting the help of a consultant in your change initiative, it is important to understand how consultants can help you, and how you can make the most of their services (see appendix B for more information on selecting a consultant).

With respect to change initiatives it's useful to think of two types of consultants:

- **Expert consultants.** They help to shape the context of change. Which strategy needs to change? Which structure? Which systems?

- **Process consultants.** They recommend processes for making change happen, and help implement them. They also coach the leadership and the change team.

Either of these types of consultants augment the organization's official leadership and generally follow this modus operandi:

1. **Diagnosis.** A team of junior consultants gathers information both inside and outside the organization with the goal of:

1) determining where the company stands in terms of some measure of organization performance, and 2) the company's problems and the root causes with respect to that performance measure.

2. **Capabilities assessment.** The capabilities of the company's human and physical resources are assessed.

3. **Strategy development.** Working with management, the consulting team develops a strategy for reaching the desired level of performance. Depending on the situation, that strategy may include various doses of employee training, process reengineering, organizational restructuring, and even some new information technology.

4. **Implementation.** Consultant teams provide training and work with employee teams to plan the change program and operationalize the strategy.

From the organization's point of view, it is generally most useful to give consultants the lead with some of these agenda items and use them in advisory roles for others. For example, a consultant is often ideally suited to conduct agenda items 1 and 2. He or she can be more objective in making a diagnosis and assessing internal capabilities than can an internal team. Also, the consultant is likely to have an intimate knowledge of industry best practices that your own people may lack.

As you move through the agenda, consultants should gradually assume background roles. Beginning with the strategy development phase, company personnel have an obligation to shoulder more and more of the burden, as shown in figure 5-1. After all, it's their program, and they'll have to live with it.

The relationship we've described is, of course, a generalized model. Different types of programs will call for different roles and relationships. Consider the Theory E and Theory O approaches we described in chapter 1 of this book. As you may recall, Theory E change is a top-down approach that focuses on restructuring the asset base of the business with the goal of producing rapid improvements in shareholder value. Such change relies heavily on consultants, who

**FIGURE 5-1**

**The Roles of Consultants and Employees in Change Programs**

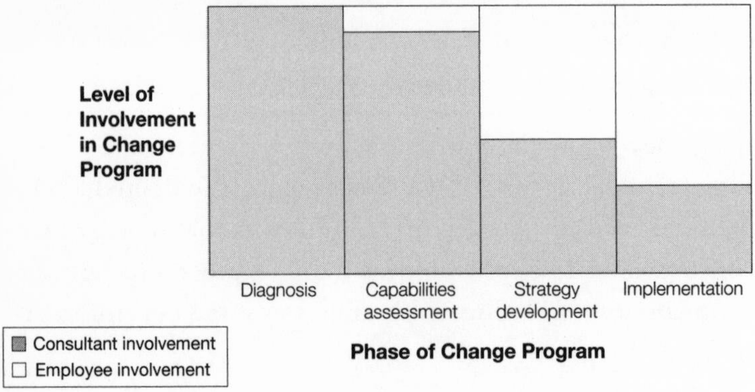


identify and analyze the problems and shape the solutions. According to authors Michael Beer and Nitin Nohria, "A SWAT team of Ivy League-educated MBAs, armed with an arsenal of state-of-the-art ideas, is brought in to find new ways to look at the business and manage it. The consultants can help CEOs get a fix on urgent issues and priorities. They also offer much-needed political and psychological support for CEOs who are under fire from financial markets."[7]

Theory O change programs, in contrast, rely far less on consultants. Instead, consultants act as expert resources who prepare and empower employees to do the heavy lifting of change, including business analysis and the crafting of solutions. This is, in effect, what happened in General Electric's famous "Work Out" initiative of the late 1980s—a prototypical Theory O change program. That program aimed to stamp out bureaucracy (which CEO Jack Welch loathed) and reshape the operating units to behave more like entrepreneurial small companies. Consultants had the job of organizing New England–style "town meetings" for each of the company's operating units. Small groups of employees were invited to these meetings, where consultants facilitated discussion between bosses and employees on how each group's business could be improved.

Thus, the best approach to using consultants is bound to be heavily situational. If the goal is restructuring, change consultants can and should play a major role—they have very specialized knowledge and experience for these rare events. But if the change involves changing how people work, put your own people in change and use consultants as facilitators.

## Summing Up

This chapter addressed the all-important phase of implementation in a change program. Without effective implementation, all the front-end analysis, strategizing, and planning will be a waste of time and money.

Six activities were identified as essential for implementation:

1. **Enlisting the support and involvement of key people.** This means assembling a team with the right blend of skills, authority, resources, and leadership.

2. **Crafting a good implementation plan.** Remember to keep it simple, flexible, divided into achievable chunks, and with clearly defined roles and responsibilities.

3. **Supporting the plan with consistent behaviors.** Make sure that management "walks the talk."

4. **Developing "enabling structures."** This means training, pilot programs, and alignment of the rewards system with your change goals.

5. **Celebrating milestones.** Identify important milestones in the project and celebrate them when they are reached.

6. **Communicating relentlessly.** Tell them why, tell them how, and tell them often.

Do these well and you'll tilt the odds of success in your favor.

The role of consultants was also discussed in this chapter. Exactly how consultants should participate is generally a function of the type of change you're aiming for.

- If the change is restructuring, with the purchase, sale, and/or consolidation of units, consultants will play a large role.

- If the change involves how people work together, company personnel should be prepared to carry the burden of leadership.

## 6

# Helping People Adapt

*Strategies to Help Reduce Stress and Anxiety*

## Key Topics Covered in This Chapter

- *The four stages of reaction to change: shock, defensive retreat, acknowledgment, and acceptance and adaptation*

- *How individuals can help themselves navigate change*

- *How managers can help employees cope with change*

- *Alternative ways for managers to think about change resisters*

T HE BUSINESS PRESS and many academics like to talk about the importance of change, and how it makes us all better people and more satisfied and fulfilled with our work. They extol the virtues of "thriving" on chaos and encourage us to "embrace" change as if it were something we just can't get enough of. You get the feeling that had they been around during the thirteenth century these writers would have described the Crusaders' sack of Constantinople as a "mutual learning experience" for the Latin West and the Byzantine East.

In reality, change puts lots of people through the wringer—particularly Theory E change that aims to quickly increase shareholder value. Far from "thriving," some employees don't survive the change program at all, let alone come out in one piece. Both unsuccessful and successful change programs produce stress, and many result in the displacement of good people. Ask the thousands of General Electric employees who lost their jobs when Jack Welch pared down his company to a manageable set of future-facing businesses. They didn't call him Neutron Jack for nothing. The same goes for "Chainsaw" Al Dunlap, who lopped off great chunks of the employment ranks at Scott Paper in a major corporate makeover. Ask the people who survived several rounds of downsizing at IBM and Cisco Systems about "embracing" change.

In these types of changes, survivors are almost universally shell-shocked. Their morale is poor, trust in the company is at rock bottom, and employee loyalty is out the window. A good manager cannot restore the world for these people, but he or she can help them through the turmoil, and get them back into a productive frame of mind. This chapter explains the stress caused by workplace change and what you can do to help people through it.

## Reactions to Change: A Sense of Loss and Anxiety

The typical employee spends at least eight hours a day doing, in general, fairly routine tasks. Indeed, when companies talk about their "culture," they imply a certain measure of stability and routine. They reinforce that stability with job descriptions that prescribe in concrete terms what employees should do day-to-day and week-to-week. There's a tangible agreement that if the employee does X, and does it well and on time, the employee will receive Y in compensation and be viewed as a company member in good standing.

There is also a psychological contract between employee and company: As long as the employee fits into work and social patterns, he or she "belongs." And there is a political dimension as well, demanding that career-minded employees attend to certain written and unwritten "rules" of the game. But what happens when the contract or rules are changed unexpectedly? Take the following case, for example:

> *This morning we got a memo addressed to "all staff." It said that year-end performance bonuses are being discontinued. Just like that—20 percent of my salary out the window! And after all the long hours I've put in during the last months. . . .*

How would you suppose this person might feel? She has definitely experienced a loss. Losses caused by change programs usually aren't as drastic as this, however. They are more likely to be a change in job description, or a perceived loss in turf, status, or self-meaning. They tend to be threats to values that someone has built up, rather than monetary losses.

Even a positive change can create anxiety for some people. For example, a person who's given a promotion may wonder: Can I handle the job? How will my friendships with people in the department be affected now that I'm their boss? Will the required travel and longer hours create problems at home?

Those questions reflect a fear of the unknown, which often accompanies a loss of certainty. For most people, however, the negative aspects of change are related to a loss of control—over their incomes and influence, their sources of pride, and how they have grown accustomed to living and working. When these factors are threatened, expect to see anxiety and anger.

## Stages in Reaction to Change

Most people eventually adapt and are reconciled to change, but not before passing through various psychological stages, which are examined here. One way to think about those stages is through the concept of risk. According to one theory, change requires people to perform or perceive in unfamiliar ways, which involves risks. Those risks potentially threaten a person's self-esteem.[1] Understandably, people are uncomfortable with risk and tend to avoid it when they can. When they cannot, however—as when they're roped into a corporate change initiative—adaptation to change tends to proceed through predictable psychological stages. In some respects, these stages resemble the grieving process a person experiences after the loss of a loved one. The four stages are:[2]

1. **Shock.** In the shock phase, people feel threatened by anticipated change. They may even deny its existence: "This isn't happening." They become immobilized and often shut down in order to protect themselves. People feel unsafe, timid, and unable to act, much less take risks. Needless to say, productivity drops during this stage.

2. **Defensive retreat.** Eventually people caught in a change vortex move from shock to defensive retreat. They get angry and lash out at what has been done to them, even as they hold on to accustomed ways of doing things. They attempt to keep a grip on the past

while decrying the fact that it's changed. This conflict likewise precludes taking risks; the situation is perceived as too unsafe.

3. **Acknowledgment.** Eventually, most people cease denying the fact of change, and acknowledge that they have lost something. They mourn. The psychological dynamics of this stage include both grief and liberation. Thus, one can feel like a pawn in a game while also being able to view that game with some degree of objectivity and psychological distance. At this point the notion of taking risks becomes more palatable and people begin to explore the pros and cons of the new situation. Each "risk" that succeeds builds confidence and prepares people for more.

4. **Acceptance and adaptation.** Most people eventually internalize the change, make any needed adaptations, and move on. They see themselves "before and after" the change and, even if it's a grudging acknowledgment, they consider the change "for the best." In some cases, people actively advocate for what they had previously opposed. Acceptance and adaptation means relinquishing the old situation, as well as the pain, confusion, and fear experienced in the earlier stages of change.

Progress through these four stages is linear and should only be accelerated with great care. Speeding up the process risks carrying unfinished psychological "baggage" from one phase to the next. Thus, if you're the manager of people going through the four-stage process you need to resist your natural bias toward action and exercise patience. The expression "time heals all" says it well enough.

This theory about how people deal with change and eventually accept it is somewhat simplistic. Although most people work through the four emotional stages—some more quickly than others—some will get stuck in defensive retreat and channel their energies into resistance.

People get stuck for two basic and obvious reasons: first, change is not a single event with neat and tidy beginnings and endings; and second, people's experiences with change vary with individual circumstance. Thus, frameworks like this one are far from perfect. To further complicate matters, change often hits from two or more directions at the same time. For example, a division of a large corporation is put through a wrenching restructuring in which many people are furloughed; the same division is then sold to another corporation, which results in new leadership and new policies. Coming all at once (or in rapid sequence), these multiple changes can severely stress or undo the anchor points of the employees and managers who remain. Agreed-upon ways of working, affiliations, skills, and self-concept slip away. When anchor points such as these are removed, most people are immobilized or thrown into a defense mode. In a worst-case scenario, the individual under siege at the office is simultaneously experiencing major change at home—a divorce, for example.

People who are emotionally fragile are at the greatest risk during change initiatives. They typically have the greatest difficulty handling feelings of loss and may choose to see themselves as victims of the process. A perception of victimhood will always hinder an employee's ability to move on after change has occurred.

## The Conventional Advice

Smart managers attempt to accelerate adaptation to change, and for understandable reasons: Employees who are preoccupied with their internal issues are not fully productive. Indeed, people in the early stages of change are often unable to do much at all. It thus makes good business sense to help them cope and move forward. Unfortunately, such good intentions are often viewed as manipulative, controlling, or autocratic. If the benefits of change are overly hyped, if there are too many pep rallies and too many "it's really good for you" assurances, people will become cynical and dig in their heels. "How can they say everything is rosy when I feel as though I've been stabbed in the back?"

So, what can you do to minimize the negative aspects of change for people in your organization? Consider the following list of conventional advice for dealing with change:

- Keep your cool in dealing with others.

- Do your best to handle pressure smoothly and effectively.

- Respond nondefensively when others disagree with you.

- Develop creative and innovative solutions to problems.

- Be willing to take risks and try out new ideas.

- Be willing to adjust priorities to changing conditions.

- Demonstrate enthusiasm for and commitment to long-term goals.

- Be open and candid when dealing with others.

- Participate actively in the change process.

- Make clear-cut decisions as needed.

This is good advice, but it fails to take into account psychological needs that must be addressed. Most people are aware of the wisdom of taking responsibility for dealing with change themselves; they recognize the importance of the "right attitude." Most people, however, do not want this shoved down their throats. Rather, they prefer some empathy, and some understanding of what they are experiencing. They are less interested in advice than in understanding and support.

The next two sections explore ways in which people facing change can help themselves and provide guidelines that managers can use to help their employees (and themselves) cope with difficult parts of the change process.


## What Individuals Can Do for Themselves

The strong emotions that most of us feel at the onset of change—anger, depression, and shock—are not useful. They neither comfort us nor move us forward. And they are often emotional. We have rational *and* emotional sides of our beings, and each must be paid its

---

### Tips for Recognizing the Emotional Side

- Remind people that anger, depression, and shock are natural reactions to loss. People need to give themselves permission to feel what they are feeling. Change always involves a loss of some kind: a job, colleagues, a role, even one's identity. That loss must be duly acknowledged and mourned.

- Let mourning take its course.

- Be patient. Recognize that time is needed to come to grips with a situation and move through the various stages. It cannot be done overnight, and no single timeline works for everyone. But don't let people wallow in self-pity and grief.

---

due. (See "Tips for Recognizing the Emotional Side.") The secret to success is to allow the emotional side to express itself—that is, to give it due recognition—but to gradually pass control to the rational side.

### Overcome Powerlessness

A feeling of powerlessness, or loss of control, is a major cause of change-related distress. Someone over whom we have no control has arbitrarily upset the routines of work, sold off the division, laid off many of our workplace friends, or altered the compensation system. Worse, we have no recourse.

One antidote to feeling powerless is to establish a sense of personal control in other areas of our lives. For example, taking charge of your investment club's monthly newsletter or designing a room addition to your house represent ways to regain a sense of personal control. Another antidote is to avoid taking on other efforts that sap energy. Thus, if adapting to change is arduous, individuals should husband their resources. This entails not only maintaining physical well-being, but nourishing your psyche. For example:

- get enough sleep

- pay attention to diet and exercise

- take occasional breaks at the office

- relax with friends

- engage in hobbies

These are not forms of escapism, nor do they distract a person from reality. Rather, they are practical ways of exerting control over one's life during a period of flux.

## Inventory the Gains and Losses

Accepting strong emotions and acknowledging the importance of patience in dealing with change are vital; but so is developing objectivity about what is happening. We have choices in how we perceive change, and we are able to develop the capacity to see benefits, not just losses, in new situations. Coming to accept and adapt to change is in fact a process of balancing: "What have I lost?" should be balanced by "What am I gaining?" This is far different than "looking on the bright side." Inventorying personal losses and gains is a tangible step that people can take in gathering the strength to move on.

## Re-anchor

"Re-anchoring" is related to inventorying gains and losses. Here, the individual balances the emotional investment in essential work-related anchor points—how work is done, affiliations, skills, self-concept in relation to the work—with emotional investments in other areas, such as family, friends, and civic and religious activities. Thus, when one or more anchor points at the workplace is uprooted, the person can remain steady by creating or strengthening anchor points elsewhere. For example, if workplace change has resulted in your transfer to a new department where you have no real friends, you could:

- develop new friendships in that department;

- join the department softball team; or

- solidify your friendships outside work—for example, by attending the Thursday night book club meeting you've skipped for the past year.

Admittedly, inventorying and re-anchoring are difficult when a person is in the grip of strong emotions. Perhaps the best mechanism for coping with change, then, is anticipating it. No one escapes the effects of change, in the workplace or elsewhere, but those who recognize that its impact will be powerful, that the process of adaptation and acceptance will take time, and that we all have other sources of strength, are much better positioned than those who are caught flat-footed.

## How Managers Can Help Employees Cope

Many managers find that addressing straightforward, technical issues in the change effort—such as the new department layout, or who gets what training—is comparatively easy. But consciously or not, they ignore the more complex and unpredictable concerns of people being changed. The rationale may be a business one: "We don't have time for that; we're here to make money." Or it may be emotional: "I don't want to get involved in messy feelings; that's not my job."

Ignoring the human side of change, however, is shortsighted and a symptom of ineffective management. Managers are paid to get things done with the human and financial resources given to them— imperfect as those resources may be. Like infantry platoon leaders in a skirmish, they must muster all the firepower at their disposal—and that means getting every one of their people engaged. They cannot afford to write off people who are too afraid to move. They have to get everyone into the fight. And that sometimes means helping them through their fear. With that thought in mind, let's consider what managers can do at each of the four stages described earlier.

## Stage One: Shock

Good managers prepare people for change long before the shock hits. Returning to our military example, military organizations don't wait until the heat of battle to deal with the shock it induces in people. Instead, they prepare soldiers for what lies ahead through rigorous training and simulations. As a manager, you, too, can prepare your people for the shock of change by periodically inoculating them with small doses of it:

- Change work processes whenever you see real opportunities for improvement.

- Give people periodic reassignments that force them to learn new things and deal with new situations.

- Use stretch goals to encourage flexibility and greater effort.

- Never allow anyone to get too comfortable in his or her job.

- Root out any sense of entitlement.

If you prepare people for change, they will experience less shock when a really big shake-up hits your unit. Preparation is probably the most important thing you can do as a change manager. Even with good preparation, however, there's bound to be shock, and you'll have to deal with the denial, "shutting down," and timidity that characterize this stage. You'll need to apply some "first aid":

- If people have had the anchors of their work lives yanked away, find new ones for them to latch onto. These may be their new roles in their new work groups.

- Provide opportunities for people to vent their feelings.

- Be a good listener, but avoid trying to sell them on the idea that things are actually better for them—they are not yet ready to hear this.

- Help your employees manage the stress that results from change (see the "Managing Stress Levels" checklist in appendix A).

## Stage Two: Defensive Retreat

People in the stage of defensive retreat get angry and lash out even as they try to hold on to the old ways of doing things. This behavior reduces their productivity. Here are a couple things you can do to get them through this stage:

- Do what you can to keep "retreaters" connected to the immediate group—the strongest anchor there is. Individuals who find themselves decoupled from their familiar social arrangements are likely to be the most damaged, since the group acts as a source of identity, safety, and support. The military, which has enormous experience in this area, emphasizes what it calls "small group cohesion." It knows that soldiers will do remarkable things as members of small, closely-knit groups (see "The Power of Small Group Cohesion"). You should do the same by helping people connect to others in their new circumstances. Group activities, lunchtime meetings, or outings all help build connections between strangers.

- Provide a verbal outlet for the grievances and the angst that needs to be vented. When management provides opportunities for grievances and frustrations to be aired constructively, employee bitterness and frustration may be diminished.

## Stage Three: Acknowledgment

Eventually, most people stop denying the fact of change and acknowledge their new situation. The psychological dynamics of this stage include both grief for what has been lost and nascent feelings of liberation. Though they continue to feel like pawns in a game controlled by others, they begin to view that game with a certain amount of distance and objectivity. Risk-taking becomes possible as people begin to explore the pros and cons of the new situation.

You can help people in this stage in several ways:

## The Power of Small Group Cohesion

Biographer/historian William Manchester was wounded during the bloody World War II battle to take the Japanese-held island of Okinawa. Although Manchester had a "ticket home" wound, he skipped out of the field hospital and rejoined his unit of U.S. Marines, who were still in the thick of combat. Many years later he recollected the motivation that propelled him to put his life on the line (again). His account underscores the power of small group cohesion—something that every change manager must appreciate:

*And then, in one of those great thundering jolts in which a man's real motives are revealed to him in an electrifying vision, I understand, at last, why I jumped hospital that Sunday thirty-five years ago, and, in violation of orders, returned to the front and almost certain death. It was an act of love. Those men on the line were my family, my home. . . . They had never let me down, and I couldn't do it to them. I had to be with them rather than to let them die and me live with the knowledge that I might have saved them. Men, I now knew, do not fight for flag or country, for the Marine Corps or glory or any other abstraction. They fight for one another.[a]*

a   William Manchester, *Goodbye Darkness* (Boston, MA: Little, Brown and Company, 1979).

- Continue your role as a sounding board for complaints and questions. Ask "How do you feel about this?" to get a fix on an individual's emotional state. But begin now to stress the benefits of the new situation.

- Build further on the "anchors" and group cohesion you established in the previous stage.

- Encourage people to try new things—to take some risks. Ask "What could we do about this?" Each risk that succeeds will build confidence and prepare people for the final stage.

### Stage Four: Acceptance and Adaptation

Most employees will eventually accept their new situation and adapt to it. Others may drift off to new jobs they find more satisfactory—either inside or outside the organization. A certain number will never adapt, however, and their performance will suffer. Here are some things you can do to facilitate this final stage:

- Keep working on group dynamics. Remember that people are generally less concerned with the tasks they are given than how they fit in with the group.

- Try to understand what each of your people needs to feel a sense of accomplishment. For one person that might be an opportunity to demonstrate her special talent for creating PowerPoint presentations. For another it could be his project management ability. For each person, find that special talent and give him or her an opportunity to use it and to earn some recognition.

- Move the focus from feelings to action. Action will take their minds off their hurt feelings and insecurity, which will eventually fade away.

- Be prepared to "outplace" those individuals who simply cannot or will not fit into the new situation. These individuals will be a permanent drag on performance and cast a negative pall over the unit.

The advice given here about listening, accepting, and supporting may seem overly simple and obvious. But it's these simple and obvious actions that change managers often overlook. Don't make the same mistake. (For an inspirational story on how one leader managed change under stressful circumstances, see "How Shackleton Did It.")

# Rethinking Resisters

Although addressed in a previous chapter, we return to the issue of change resistance here since such resistance is a natural human response—one with which managers must learn to cope.

"Resister" typically describes anyone who refuses to accept the change, or who doesn't change as fast as we do. As such, a resister is considered an obstacle to be overcome. Those labeled resisters are viewed as people with poor attitudes, or lacking in team spirit. But treating resisters this way serves only to intensify real resistance, thereby thwarting or at least sidetracking the possibility of change.

Resistance is a part of the natural process of adaptation to change—a normal response of those who have a strong interest in maintaining the current state and guarding themselves against loss. "Why should I give up what has created meaning for me?" they ask. "What do I get in its place?"

Resistance is generally more complicated than "I won't." It is a much more painful question: "Why should I?" Once resistance is understood as a natural reaction—part of a process—it can be viewed more objectively as a step in the process that leads to acceptance and adaptation. At the very minimum, resistance denotes energy—energy that can be worked with and redirected. The strength of resistance, moreover, indicates the degree to which change has touched on something valuable to an individual or the overall organization. Discovering what that valuable something is can help you manage the change effort. One theorist puts it this way:

> First, [the resisters] are the ones most apt to perceive and point out real threats, if such exist, to the well-being of the system, which may be the unanticipated consequences of projected changes. Second, they are especially apt to react against any change that might reduce the integrity of the system. Third, they are sensitive to any indication that those seeking change fail to understand or identify with the core values of the system they seek to influence.[3]

Thus, resisters may provide important information, and dismissing them as naysayers may be a genuine error.

In summary, rethinking resistance to change means seeing it as a normal part of adaptation, something most of us do to protect ourselves. It is a potential source of energy, as well as information about the change effort and direction. So, instead of viewing all resistance as an obstacle, try to understand its sources, motives, and potentially affirmative core. Doing so can open up possibilities for realizing change.

## How Shackleton Did It

Thanks to many books and films produced over the past few years, most readers are probably familiar with the ill-fated Antarctic expedition of Sir Ernest Shackleton and his ship, *Endurance*. Though he utterly failed to accomplish his intended goal, Shackleton's success in holding his crew together, and in returning all to safety, has made him quite a hero. Much can be learned from his management and leadership in that period of extreme adversity.

The *Endurance* left England in 1914 with the goal of landing on the Antarctic shore and sending a team of men and dogs to the other side of the continent by way of the Pole—a feat that had not yet been accomplished. But Shackleton never made it to the staging area. Trapped by an ice pack in the Weddell Sea and unable to move, ship and crew were forced to stay put for almost fifteen months until the ice broke up. How Shackleton held his team together and kept them alive and healthy during that time in the world's most inhospitable environment provides insights into change management.

Like employees in a change situation over which they had no control, the *Endurance* crew saw that the goal they had enlisted for was abandoned. Everything they had hoped for and had prepared for had to be scratched. They were out of communication with the world they knew and could expect neither help nor rescue from any quarter. When the pressures of the ice eventually crushed the sides of the ship, slow starvation or death from exposure became highly probable.

How did their leader keep the expedition's members from mentally and physically shutting down under these circumstances? Here are three actions taken by Shackleton that proved effective:

- **He immediately provided a new and acceptable goal.** The crew would live on the ice pack until it broke up; they would then navigate to safety via the ship's lifeboats. As long as people had a worthy goal to work toward, their energies and spirits were maintained.

- **He kept everyone busy.**  Fifteen months on an ice floe could have driven the crew to fratricide. So Shackleton made sure that everyone kept busy. Meteorological data was recorded daily. Regular soccer matches and dogsled races between teams supported group cohesion and maintained mental and physical health. A drama group was created to perform theatrical entertainment. Until the ship was eventually crushed, crewmembers tended to necessary repairs. A core team planned for the eventual voyage by lifeboat. Holidays were celebrated.

- **Difficult and undesirable chores were equally shared.**  Shackleton, the ship's captain, and other leaders lived and worked with everyone else. There was no sense of "them" and "us." They were in it together.

In April, 1916, the ice floe on which the crew had survived for more than a year began to break apart. Lifeboats crammed with men and supplies were launched into the frigid sea—the first leg of a long and harrowing journey toward safety. And despite months of continued hardship and peril, every member of the Shackleton expedition survived and—together—returned safely to England.

## Summing Up

This chapter described how people react to change and how managers can effectively deal with negative reactions. Here are some key points to remember:

- People faced with dramatic change generally respond through four stages: shock, defensive retreat, acknowledgment, and acceptance and adaptation. These stages are similar to the grieving process that follows the loss of a friend or family member. Your challenge as a change manager is to patiently help people through these stages.

- Individuals can overcome some of the emotional problems associated with change by: overcoming the powerlessness they feel by developing a sense of personal control over other areas of their lives; gaining greater objectivity of their situations by making an inventory of personal losses and gains; and "re-anchoring" themselves.

- Managers can help people through the four stages using a number of methods, which include listening, keeping people as connected as possible to their work groups or other routines, and eventually moving them from a focus on personal emotions to a focus on productive activities.

# 7

# Crisis Resolution

## The Road to Recovery

## Key Topics Covered in This Chapter

- *The importance of moving quickly and decisively*

- *The role of communications*

- *How project management techniques can help in crisis resolution*

- *Why strong leadership matters*

I F   Y O U ' V E   F O L L O W E D   the rules of containment offered earlier, your company will be in a much better position to resolve its crisis. Fast and effective action on the containment front will result in a crisis that is smaller and more manageable. The containment effort will also assure that the true problem and its dimensions are correctly identified. Otherwise, crisis resolution will be fighting the wrong battle. Beyond the containment phase, the job of the crisis management team is to keep on top of the problem and not let up until it is resolved and the situation has returned to normalcy.

This chapter will take you through the many things the crisis management team must do to bring about a resolution.

## Move Quickly

Time is not your friend during a crisis. As in the containment phase, time only gives the problem an opportunity to spread and take root, making it more intractable. The containment effort is a holding action at best; delay in working toward a resolution provides opportunities for the crisis to break through that holding action. Consider this hypothetical news report:

*As the strike against Amalgamated Hat Racks enters its third week, a nationwide boycott of Amalgamated's products appears to be taking shape. Jessie Jamison, a spokesperson for the striking union, announced today that union members across the country are being asked to boycott all Amalgamated outlets and products. "In all likelihood," said Jamison, "we'll have pickets around the company's retail stores in Toronto, Boston, Los Angeles, and Santa Fe by this time next week."*

A long-lasting crisis may also imprint the public consciousness with a negative view of the company. If the morning newspaper reports your company's travails day after day and week after week, the public will associate the company with trouble and conflict for years to come. Microsoft's long-running battle with the U.S. Department of Justice over whether it was guilty of monopolistic practices—and subsequent battles with several state prosecutors—certainly had that

---

## Tips for Relieving Crisis Stress

If you are on a crisis management team, you will feel lots of pressure. The pace is fast. The stakes are high—for the company, for your fellow employees, and for you personally. Because your control of the facts is incomplete, you know that mistakes are easy to make. Fear is in the air. The people around you are nervous and unsettled, and their emotions are bound to infect you.

Here are a few tips for relieving the stress:

- Get enough sleep.

- Take a break and do anything that will dissipate the tension building up inside you: a long walk in the woods, a bike ride along the seashore. If you play a musical instrument, play a few tunes every day.

- Don't fixate on what could go wrong. Instead, look at risks objectively, and then shift your focus to the benefits of making things go right.

- Avoid a bunker mentality. Spend more time with "normal" people—i.e., people who are not in the midst of a crisis.

Remember that some tension is good; it will keep you focused and keep your energy level up. Too much tension, on the other hand, may paralyze your ability to think and act.

effect. The public was treated to regular reports of Microsoft's alleged sins. Even those found later to be groundless surely had an impact on the public's attitude toward the software giant.

Equally bad, it's unlikely that your business will operate at peak efficiency as long as the crisis continues. Suppliers and customers will be wary. Employee defections will increase, and recruiting efforts will be more difficult. Employees will waste time as they worry about their jobs or speculate among themselves about the company's problems. The antidote to these negative effects is to resolve the crisis as quickly as possible.

## Gather Facts Continually

Crises are often dynamic events, mutating on their own or in response to the action of participants. You may begin resolution efforts with a very clear picture of the problems and the forces arrayed against you. That picture is likely to change in response to whatever actions you take or fail to take. Also, new information will become available during every day of the crisis.

The remedy to both problems—incomplete information and a shifting situation—is to continually gather and process facts about the crisis as you attempt to resolve it. Make "What new things have we learned today?" part of daily crisis team meetings. Adopt a sense-and-respond model in which you are continually adapting to new information. To do otherwise—that is, to hold to a plan based on initial facts—can only assure failure.

## Communicate Relentlessly

Communication is one of the crisis team's most essential tools. Telling the company's story provides important information for key constituents, including customers, suppliers, shareholders, and employees. Communication is also a means of suppressing rumors and coordinating the many activities required to resolve the crisis. For

## Tips for Communicating During a Crisis

- Be candid.

- Give the facts.

- Be honest about what you know *and* what you don't know.

- Set up a rumor control hot line.

- Record a voice message on the company information line every day with the latest information.

- Don't speculate.

example, in the aftermath of a fire or storm, employees must be told when and where to report for work and what they should do. If the information system is down for the count, someone must notify creditors that their payments may be late. If picket lines are preventing the production facility from filling customer orders, those customers should hear from you. If news reporters are knocking on the door, you must have a strategy for getting your side of the story across and making it resonate with the public.

If you've created a communication plan as part of normal contingency planning, as recommended earlier, you'll be ready for most eventualities in this area. If you have not, appropriate members of the crisis management team should quickly develop one.

### Document Your Actions

Document your sources of information as well as your decisions, intentions, and actions throughout the course of crisis resolution. You may question the value of that advice. After all, how many generals ask their staffs to chronicle their campaigns as they happen? Who has the time when so much is happening around them?

In fact, military organizations do chronicle their decisions and actions. Doing so provides a record from which after-action lessons can be drawn. At the beginning of World War II, for example, the U.S. Navy assigned Harvard historian Samuel Eliot Morison, a high-ranking naval reserve officer, to the task of chronicling the war at sea from beginning to end. Morison, in turn, recruited a staff of researchers to help with the project. Their collective effort produced a fifteen-volume work from which the next two generations of naval students, strategists, and tacticians would draw important lessons.

Documenting your situation and actions will have similar value in the aftermath of crisis, when the crisis team and others attempt to learn what went well, what went badly, and how they can improve in the future. Documentation will also be helpful in any subsequent legal actions.

## Use Project Management Techniques When Appropriate

The difficulties you face in resolving a crisis may be qualitatively similar to the challenges you face in other areas of your business. Examples include launching a new product into a new market, reorganizing an operating unit, and building an e-commerce function. Such challenges are often addressed through formal project teams. Crises and projects share several important characteristics:

- They are nonroutine, rarely repeating activities.

- They require the skills and experience of people from many different functions.

- They are not scheduled to continue indefinitely but are to be resolved at some future date.

- Participants return to their regular duties once the job is finished.

Those characteristics suggest that crisis teams should organize themselves and attack problems as project teams already do with considerable success. That means bringing together the experiences, authority, and skills needed to gain control of the situation. However, there are some notable differences. Crisis teams, unlike project teams, do not always have the luxury of time in which to plan their work. Teams formed around specific threats identified through risk auditing (e.g., fire, flood, or a breakdown of IT systems) have contingency plans, and many have used simulations to train. But even these lack certain knowledge of what must be done because crises often evolve in unpredictable ways. Nevertheless, there are enough similarities to encourage crisis managers to take a page from the project manager's book.

Project management has four essential phases: defining and organizing, planning, managing execution, and closing down the project. Let's consider how crisis managers can adapt those steps to their own challenges.

## Defining and Organizing

The tasks involved in the first phase are to clearly define the project's objectives and to organize the right people and resources around them. Whether crisis managers are facing a product recall or the aftermath of a disastrous fire, they can do the same, asking "What—exactly—is the problem? What must we do to resolve it? Who should we enlist to help us? What resources will we need to solve the problem and return our situation to normal?"

If you define the crisis correctly and organize the right set of people and resource around it, you will have made an excellent beginning.

## Planning

Planning begins with the objective and works backward in four successive steps:

1. Identifying each of the many tasks that must be done

2. Identifying the individuals or groups best qualified to accomplish each task

3. Estimating the time required to complete each task

4. Scheduling all tasks in the right order

If fire damage to your office building is the source of crisis, your objective might be three-fold: secure temporary office space for dislocated workers as needed; restore the damaged space to working order; and communicate regularly with affected personnel. Approached from a project management perspective, each of those objectives would then be broken down into a necessary set of tasks and subtasks. For example, to restore the damaged space you might identify the following tasks and estimate the time required to complete them:

- Obtain a complete evaluation of the fire damage and itemized list of necessary repairs (fourteen days).

- Negotiate with and hire a contractor to do the repairs (fourteen days).

- Work with an office-furniture supplier and technology vendor to refit the repaired space (thirty days).

- Oversee the contractor's reconstruction work (eighteen days).

- Communicate with employees about building restoration progress (ongoing).

Some of those tasks must be tackled in a sequence; for example, you cannot negotiate with a contractor until the damages have been assessed. Other tasks can be handled in parallel; for example, you can be working with an office-furniture supplier even as repairs are being made.

The planning process must also assign responsibility for each task to a specific individual. Assigning individual responsibility is your best assurance that tasks will be done and done well. If no one in particular owns a task, it probably won't be done on time or to your satisfaction.

**Managing Execution**

The managing execution phase requires all the traditional chores of effective management as well as careful monitoring and control. Together, they assure adherence to the plan, standards, and the budget. The budget is rarely an issue during a crisis. The company is usually taking such a financial beating that the cost of efforts to stem the losses and get things back on track pales by comparison. Monitoring and control, however, remain critical. Always ask these questions:

- Are all planned tasks under way?

- Are all tasks on schedule, or have some hit obstacles?

- Are the company's messages to employees, the media, and other stakeholders accurate and consistent?

Project leaders spend most of their time coordinating the efforts of their teams. Crisis team leaders must do the same. They need everyone working together and at a high level of energy to defeat the crisis.

Just a reminder: The tools of project management are not appropriate in resolving all crises. A deepening financial crisis is one; a case of fraud or embezzlement is another. However, when a damaging event hits and quickly ends—as in a fire, a paralyzing blizzard, or a product recall—project management tools can help you pick up the pieces and return operations to normal in an orderly way.

### Closing Down the Project

One common feature of projects and crises is that they eventually end. The end of a project is the point at which its objectives are achieved. The new product line is launched. The new e-commerce Web site is up and running successfully. The company's move to a new headquarters is finished, and the pace of business has returned to normal. A project terminates when its objectives are met, but that happens only after wrapping up loose ends and reflecting on the lessons learned from the project.

Crisis management likewise has a final, wrap-up phase, and one of the main tasks of that phase is to look back on the experience and draw out its lessons: What went right? What did we do wrong? How would we change our approach if and when another similar crisis hits the company? The learning issue will be addressed in detail later. The points to remember here are that the crisis team must

## Don't Play the Blame Game

As a crisis heats up and people try to determine what went wrong, the impulse to blame someone becomes almost irresistible. Certainly, a team member's incompetence or serious error may have caused the crisis. In the meltdown of Enron, for example, fingers pointed to Chief Financial Officer Andrew Fastow and Chairman and CEO Kenneth Lay. Finger-pointing, however, did nothing to rescue the company, save the jobs of thousands of honest and competent employees, or salvage the equity of shareholders. Energy spent on finding a villain or scapegoat is counterproductive during a crisis period. It lowers morale and stifles the creativity and commitment you need to solve the problem. So instead of playing the blame game, create an atmosphere in which people look forward to what needs to be done, not backward to who was at fault. There will be plenty of time in the aftermath to deal with blame.

- declare an official end to the crisis—but do not be premature;

- document everything significant that happened;

- get participants to participate in a postmortem, which is your best assurance that the organization will learn from its expensive experience.

## Be a Leader

During periods of crisis, people look to a strong leader. They don't look to committees or to teams as much as to a confident, visibly engaged leader to pull them through the fray. This is why military commanders mingle with their troops on the front lines of battles. This is why Winston Churchill was so often seen on the streets of London during the terrifying weeks of the blitz. This is why Lee

Iacocca, during the 1980s campaign to save Chrysler Corporation from extinction, made himself into a household name in North America. Iacocca seemed to be everywhere as he struggled to secure government guarantees for the loans Chrysler needed to rebuild itself. It seemed that wherever you turned—from the evening news, to *BusinessWeek*, to a series of television ads—Iacocca was there, telling people why a renewed Chrysler Corporation was good for jobs, the economy, and American competitiveness. Leaders like Iacocca who demonstrate strength, commitment, and confidence infect others with the same qualities.

The importance of leader visibility cannot be overstated. In his study of the 9/11 tragedy in New York City, Paul Argenti found that the most effective crisis managers displayed high levels of visibility.

> *They understood that a central part of their job is political and that their employees are, in a very real sense, their constituents. In periods of upheaval, workers want concrete evidence that top management views their distress as one of the company's key concerns. Written statements have their place, but oral statements and the sound of an empathetic human voice communicate sincerity. And if the voice belongs to a company leader, the listener has reason to think that the full weight of the company stands behind whatever promises or assurances are being made.*[1]

Perhaps no contemporary leader provided the level of visibility advocated by Argenti more effectively than New York City's former mayor, Rudolph Giuliani. Giuliani appeared at the scene of the 9/11 attacks within minutes, where he took charge of rescue operations. After the Twin Towers fell, he remained on the scene. The man seemed to be everywhere: at press conferences, at a string of funeral services, at the crisis command center, on phone interviews, talking with people on the street. As Argenti put it, "[Giuliani's] visibility, combined with his decisiveness, candor, and compassion, lifted the spirits of all New Yorkers—indeed, of all Americans."[2]

If it's your lot to lead during a crisis, play your part well. Whether you are the CEO of a large corporation or a department supervisor, find out as quickly as possible what the real problem is. Sift through the rumors, hearsay, and irrelevant information until you find the

## When Leadership Is the Problem

Current leadership is the problem in some situations. This was the case in 1999 when an investigation revealed that the Salt Lake Olympic Committee (SLOC) was involved in a network of corruption. Its members had allegedly supplied thirteen International Olympic Committee (IOC) members with scholarships, cash, and various lavish gifts in return for their votes to award the 2002 Winter Olympics to Salt Lake City, Utah. Of the thirteen, four resigned from the IOC, five were suspended, and one was given a warning. The other two members of the Salt Lake City group, the president/CEO and the vice president, also resigned. The SLOC scandal rocked the world of Olympic sports and threatened the 2002 Winter Games. It was the most serious crisis faced by any modern Olympic event.

With its leadership banished and its reputation deeply tarnished, raising the $1.4 billion in private funding needed to host the games would be extremely difficult. Wisely, Utah's governor appointed an outsider—Boston-area businessman Mitt Romney—to assume leadership and reverse the SLOC's flagging fortunes. Romney was a new face and was untainted by the problems associated with his predecessors. He was also a successful venture capitalist and business consultant with experience in turning around troubled companies. Better still, he had exactly what the SLOC lacked, a reputation for effectiveness and high ethical standards. That reputation was needed to attract the private funding and volunteers needed to make the 2002 Winter Games a success.

Romney's success in steering the SLOC out of its crisis and putting on a successful and memorable ten days of winter sporting events is a clear reminder of the importance of effective and respected leadership during crisis. If a distressed organization lacks that kind of leadership, it must dismiss its current leaders and bring in others.

truth. You can do that by asking the right people, listening to the most reliable voices, and going to the right places. And once you know the truth, respond by

- Being visible—demonstrating that someone is in charge and working to make things better

- Facing the crisis—turning fear into positive action

- Being vigilant—watching for new developments and recognizing the importance of new information

- Maintaining a focus on the company's priorities—ensuring that people are safe first, and then addressing the next most critical needs

- Assessing and responding to what is in your control—and ignoring what is not

- Breaking the rules when necessary—rules, budgets, and policies are seldom made with crises in mind

And don't forget to get people working together. A leader has the power to draw people together to act as a team. The very fact that they are doing something useful will help relieve tension, reduce fear, and resolve the crisis. Consider this example:

*A catalog retailer offered a large number of custom products—monogrammed bags, sweaters, and so forth—in its holiday catalog. But it totally underestimated the response. From the moment the catalog was released in October, the company's phone lines were swamped with orders. The company found itself in an unusual crisis: It was buried under a mountain of orders that had to be processed and shipped in time for the holidays. It hired temporary workers to help with the laborious job of customizing and shipping, but not enough reliable temps were available to deal with the order backlog.*

*The head of distribution recognized that if they didn't get everything shipped in time for Christmas, there might not be a next season. So the CEO put out a call for help. He recruited managers and staff personnel to work evening shifts in the warehouse—after they had done their regular jobs. This was a hardship for many, especially for those who had children at home. But the CEO did such a good job of explaining the details and gravity of the situation, and how their contributions would help resolve it, that most people volunteered for two or three evening shifts each week.*

*Everyone—from the CEO down—worked together for six long and grueling weeks. And their extraordinary team effort got the job done. The company enjoyed an astonishing 80 percent growth in sales that year. What could have been a crisis and failure was turned around by teamwork. And leadership made it possible.*

Getting people back into their normal routines can be one of the most important contributions a leader can make. Returning to work has many therapeutic effects. It takes the edge off the anxiety that employees experience when they have nothing to do but sit, wait, and wonder. It eliminates opportunities for idle speculation, gossip, and rumors. (Remember, idle hands *are* the devil's workshop.) Most important, it gives people a real feeling that they are part of the solution and that they are making things better.

## Declare the End of the Crisis

At some point, a crisis must come to an end. But at what point does one declare that it's over? For long-struggling and bankrupt Polaroid Corporation, the innovator of instant photography, its crisis ended in July 2002, when an affiliate of One Equity Partners acquired the company's assets. The end of other business crises are less clear cut. For example, Malden Mills, a family-owned textile producer and developer of Polartec, declared bankruptcy in November 2001 after years of struggling against overseas competition. The owner, Aaron Feuerstein, won a reprieve for his company in late 2003 by engineering a financing arrangement with a real estate development company. In return for a sizable cash infusion to the business, the developer would be able to build six hundred units of rental housing on surplus property owned by Malden Mills. It would also share ownership of the company with Feuerstein. But the crisis wasn't entirely over. Feuerstein would have to find more than $100 million to buy out the developer's interest and get his company back. The first stage of Malden Mills's crisis had ended, but a second had begun.

How can you tell when a crisis is over? Look for these signs:

- Employees are back to their normal routines.

- Customers and suppliers have the confidence they need to do business with your company.

- The telephone rings and it is *not* a news reporter.

- Sales, earnings, and other metrics of business performance are back on track.

Those are signs that the crisis is over and that management can redirect its attention to its primary responsibilities: growth and profits.

## Summing Up

- Time is not your friend during a crisis. Every day that a crisis continues creates a negative image for the company and provides opportunities for that image to spread. So once you've contained the crisis, move quickly and decisively to resolve it.

- The facts of the crisis will change as it is resolved. So continue to gather information. Doing so will keep a clear picture of the situation in front of the crisis team.

- Relentless communication will provide information to key stakeholders and suppress rumors and speculation.

- Document the crisis and its resolution as you move forward; doing so will make it possible to later evaluate the crisis team's performance and to learn from the experience.

- Many crises can be resolved using crisis management techniques, which include defining the objective, planning, managing execution, and closing down the project.

- People look to leaders for strong, confident, and visible leadership during periods of crisis.

# 8

# Learning from Your Experience

*Gather Lessons Where*
*You Find Them*

## Key Topics Covered in This Chapter

- *Declaring the end of the crisis*

- *Building a document log from which people can learn*

- *Learning from crises and putting that learning to work*

W HEN A PERSON with money crosses paths with a person with experience, the experienced person usually comes away with the money, and the other person comes away with an experience. Something similar happens during an organizational crisis. Experience has a large price tag. Even the best-managed crisis can cost millions. Johnson & Johnson's experience in the Tylenol case probably cost it some $700 million (in 2003 dollars). But in return for its pain the company received the benefit of experience—if it was alert and eager to learn. And that experience may pay important future dividends. Consider these examples:[1]

- Measures adopted by World Trade Center tenants after the first band of terrorists set off a powerful car bomb in one of the towers' underground parking lots in 1993 are credited with saving many lives eight years later, when terrorists struck again.

- Hurricane Andrew hit Florida's coast in 1992, causing a record $16.8 billion in insurance claims—the highest recorded losses from a natural disaster in U.S. history. The unprecedented claims encouraged U.S. insurance companies to rethink their approach to risk-sharing and to find ways to reduce their exposure.

This chapter provides useful tips on closing down a crisis team. It also explains how you can learn from crises and use that learning to avoid and/or prepare for future situations.

## Mark the End of the Crisis

At some point, someone in authority must declare that the crisis is over and that a crisis mind-set is no longer appropriate. That point is determined entirely by the circumstances. Here are a few examples:

- You've fended off a hostile takeover, or you've just been gobbled up by Predator Conglomerate, Inc. In either case, the crisis is over.

- The antimonopoly lawsuit that threatened to split your company into separate parts has failed, ending the crisis.

- The laptop computers that randomly burst into flames in people's briefcases have all been recalled and replaced with a safer model. End of crisis.

- The CEO has been found guilty of embezzlement and sentenced to three years in prison, where he will be teaching a course on business ethics. So ends an embarrassing chapter of company history.

Trials and tribulations eventually come to an end—for better or worse. The problem is resolved, and life returns to normal. Management must recognize and communicate this transition from crisis to normalcy.

Momentous events require a sense of closure, and business crises are no different. The organizational leader should provide such closure through a companywide meeting, a Web broadcast, or some other appropriate means. In a small or medium-sized company, the leader should visit every work group. Whichever the method, the leader should:

- Recap the crisis by explaining what happened and why it happened

- Provide a clear and candid picture of how things have been resolved; do not gloss over the losses or attempt to put a prettier face on the outcome than reality allows

- Let everyone know how things stand as of today

- Offer a plan for getting back to work and moving forward

- Remind people of the company's strategic goals

- Encourage everyone to do his or her best in moving forward

If the company has come out of its crisis without too much damage—or with a victory—consider some form of celebration: a catered lunch, a company outing, or an afternoon off for all employees. And be sure to thank the people who helped the company weather the storm. Celebrating, however, is not appropriate if anyone was hurt or killed during the crisis; a memorial service may be more suitable.

## Record the Crisis Response

Every crisis produces a record. The value of documenting the crisis and the response was noted earlier. Depending on the situation, documentation might include:

- A notice of noncompliance from a government regulatory agency

- Test data on a product alleged to have caused harm

- The crisis action plan

- A log of actions taken

- Copies of press releases

- Newspaper clippings

- A list of crisis team members and other participants

- The minutes of the crisis management team's meetings

- A stack of paid invoices for costs incurred because of the crisis

- A formal after-action damage assessment

Those documents are part of the historical record; they should be collected and stored.

Why bother with documentation, especially when the whole company is eager to put the past behind it and get back to business? The reason is that documentation is a source of learning, and learning is what makes organizations stronger. Consider this example:

> *It has been six years since a major winter storm last paralyzed the town of Wyethburg, hometown of Technodigit Products. That storm caused a five-day closure of the company's office headquarters and manufacturing plant, resulting in lost revenues, severely delayed order fulfillment, and huge overtime costs in the weeks that followed.*
>
> *Today, Technodigit has a new cast of characters. Its CEO and many senior managers have been recruited from the outside, and few who helped manage the last snow crisis are still employed by the company. Institutional memory has faded with the years.*
>
> *With winter approaching, the company's chief operating officer is eager to prepare for the worst. Must he develop a crisis management plan from scratch? Fortunately, no. A secretary who worked for the COO's predecessor at the time of the last snow emergency has brought him some gratifying news. "We have a big file around here somewhere," she tells him. "Someone kept a record of everything that happened during the blizzard of '98. I'll try to find it."*
>
> *An hour later the secretary delivers a three-ring binder and a box of documents. It contained items that will make the COO's job easier, including the 1998 snow crisis action plan and a postmortem describing everything that worked well and worked poorly—with suggestions for plan improvement.*

The executive in this story was spared lots of hard work thanks to documentation done by an earlier crisis team. Best of all, he gained the experience of people who had faced a similar crisis in the same location. Your crisis team may likewise be a gold mine of useful information during future crises—but only if you gather together all important documents and store them in accessible formats.

## Capture the Lessons Learned

Many companies spend thousands of people-hours on planning and millions of dollars on implementing but very little time reflecting on what they have done. They don't approach learning in a systematic way. Consequently, they lose much of the value that comes with experience. Not every organization is this shortsighted. The U.S. Army has maintained its Center for Army Lessons Learned for decades. The center's mission is to learn whatever it can from every type of combat operation and turn that learning into practical advice that it then disseminates to soldiers in the field. It actively solicits input from battle-tested soldiers on everything from urban warfare maneuvers, to when and when not to wear body armor, to the effectiveness of high-tech systems under adverse field conditions as experienced in mountainous Afghanistan.

The center also looks outside the army's own experience for important lessons. One article on its Web site, for example, documented and evaluated the tactics used by Chechen rebels in the embattled city of Grozny and the problems that Russian forces had in dealing with those insurgents.

Most businesspeople believe that they are light-years ahead of the military in matters of management. But lessons learned is one area in which private industry can learn a lesson of its own. And plenty of those lessons can be found in crisis management team operations and their supporting reports.

Lessons learned should be part of every crisis closedown operation. Participants should convene to identify what went right and what went wrong. This should happen as soon as possible after the crisis has passed, while memories are fresh. Participants should make a list of their successes, their failures, their unjustified assumptions, and things that could have been done better. That list should become part of the documented record.

Here is a partial list of questions that should be addressed at a lessons learned session:

- Given what we knew at the time, could the crisis have been avoided? How?

- What were the early warning signs of crisis?

- Could we have recognized the signs earlier? How?

- Which warning signals were ignored? Which were heeded? (Explain each response.)

- At what point did we realize that we faced a crisis?

- To what extent were we prepared with contingency plans or a crisis team?

- Did we have a solid plan, or did we rely on improvisation?

- Did we have the right people on the team? If not, who should have been included?

- What was the nature of our communications to different audiences? How effective were those communications?

- How effective was our public spokesperson?

- Was our leadership highly visible?

- Were our responses timely and adequate for the situation?

- What did we do right? What could we have done better?

- Which were our biggest mistakes?

- Knowing what we know now, how can we prevent the same type of crisis from occurring again?

- And the ultimate question: If we could replay this entire event, what would we do differently?

Those questions should not be asked to punish or to allocate blame, but to evaluate the performance of the response team and to prepare the organization for the future. Gather input from everyone who participated in a meaningful way. You need everyone's story, but pay particular attention to those people with expertise in the areas of importance.

Once you've gathered answers to those questions, draw out the lessons. Most should be obvious. Then record them in a systematic

TABLE 8-1

## Lessons Learned: Blizzard of 2004 Plant Closing

|  | What Worked | What Didn't Work | Ways to Improve |
|---|---|---|---|
| **Precrisis planning** | • Had most of the right people on the team<br>• Knew whom to call<br>• Supervisors knew what to do | • Part of the weather emergency plan was outdated<br>• Took too long to get organized<br>• Waited too long to send people home because CEO could not be reached; result: many caught on snow-covered roads<br>• Plan failed to include a snowplowing contract; result: all plows were busy when we most needed them. | • Update plan every six months<br>• Contract for emergency snow-plows far in advance<br>• Simulate a weather emergency each year<br>• Empower COO or head of HR to act in CEO's absence |
| **Warning signs** | • Made decisions quickly once the blizzard potential was obvious | • Didn't check forecast hourly<br>• Didn't notice that other businesses in town had already sent people home | • Pay closer attention to forecasts |
| **Communi-cations** | • Good communi-cations with employees; they knew when to leave and when to return | • Customers were left out of the loop; many could not get information on their orders for six days | • Put a self-serve order-status facility on the Web site<br>• Refer customers to the site through the recorded emer-gency message |

list grouped by topic (e.g., precrisis preparedness, warning signs, communications, execution, etc.) and organized in a form similar to table 8-1. Make this list available to all subsequent project teams.

Note: You can identify lessons about communications management by using the "Gathering and Sharing Information" worksheet found in appendix A. It will help you collect and summarize the information your team needs to be effective in a future crisis situation.

## Putting Learning to Work

Once you have drawn out the lessons of a crisis, integrate them with your plans and practices. One way to do that is to establish continuity within crisis-planning and crisis management teams. For example, if the company has just experienced a major fire, make sure that several veterans of that crisis are assigned to any subsequent crisis management team (assuming they have the right skills and performed well). These veterans will bring the experience of that earlier crisis with them and will be sources of knowledge for less experienced team members. This is the very same method used by airlines, which pair more experienced pilots with less experienced copilots.

Business crises are usually costly. Even in the best cases they throw a monkey wrench into operations and unsettle employees and customers. The worst cases can cost billions. The only good thing you can say is that they provide opportunities to learn. Make the most of these learning opportunities, and you may be able to avoid or better handle the next crisis that comes your way.

## Summing Up

- The leader should provide closure to the crisis, thereby signaling that a state of normalcy has resumed. People need closure before they can move forward.

- Thank people for their help and their patience during the crisis. If the outcome was not too damaging, celebrate the crisis's end.

- Create a file of all materials relevant to the crisis. Documentation creates a record for future learning.

- At the end of the crisis, use an informal meeting to get people talking about what went right, what went wrong, and what could have been handled more effectively. Make a systematic list of these learning points.

# *Useful Implementation Tools*

This appendix contains four forms that you may find useful at various times during a change initiative. All are adapted from Harvard ManageMentor®, an online help source for subscribers. For interactive versions of these forms, please visit www.elearning.hbsp .org/businesstools. Here's a list of the diagnostic tests, checklists, and worksheets found in this appendix:

1. **Self–Evaluation: Characteristics of Effective Leadership.** Use this form to evaluate your own leadership capabilities. Change programs require leadership at all levels.

2. **Managing Stress Levels.** This checklist is a helpful tool for identifying and managing stress among the people you deal with.

3. **Focus and Synergy.** This checklist will help you identify obstacles encountered in the change process. Use this form or something like it to keep your team focused on the most important problems. For each obstacle to your team's progress, list and evaluate options for overcoming it. Also list any allies, additional resources, or special training your team members will need in order to collaborate most effectively on the chosen option.

4. **Gathering and Sharing Information.** This checklist can help you in the all-important business of communicating, which must be done regularly and through different channels during a change initiative. Use this form to collect and summarize the information your team needs to be effective and to change.

## Self-Evaluation: Characteristics of Effective Leadership

*The questions below relate to characteristics of effective leaders. Use the questions to evaluate whether you possess these characteristics. Use the results to see where you might focus to strengthen your leadership skills.*

| Characteristics of Effective Leaders | Yes | No |
|---|---|---|
| **Caring** | | |
| 1. Do you empathize with other people's needs, concerns, and goals? | | |
| 2. Would staff members confirm that you show such empathy? | | |
| **Comfort with ambiguity** | | |
| 3. Are you willing to take calculated risks? | | |
| 4. Are you comfortable with a certain level of disruption and conflict? | | |
| **Persistent; tenacious** | | |
| 5. When pursuing a goal, do you maintain a positive, focused attitude, despite obstacles? | | |
| **Excellent communicators** | | |
| 6. Do you listen closely (rather than have a response ready before the other person finishes)? | | |
| 7. Are you comfortable running meetings? | | |
| 8. Are you comfortable making presentations and speaking in public? | | |
| 9. Do you have the skills needed to negotiate in a variety of settings? | | |
| **Politically astute** | | |
| 10. Could you diagram for yourself your organization's power structure? | | |
| 11. Can you articulate the concerns of your organization's most powerful groups? | | |
| 12. Can you identify those individuals within your organization that will support you when needed? | | |
| 13. Do you know where to turn for the resources you need? | | |
| **Able to use humor** | | |
| 14. Do you know how to use humor to relieve tense or uncomfortable situations? | | |
| **Levelheaded** | | |
| 15. In situations that are full of turmoil and confusion, do you stay calm and levelheaded? | | |

| Characteristics of Effective Leaders | Yes | No |
|---|---|---|
| **Self-aware** | | |
| 16. Are you aware/can you describe how your own patterns of behavior impact others? | | |

*If you answered "yes" to most of these questions, you have the characteristics of an effective leader.*

*If you answered "no" to some or many of these questions, you may want to consider how you can further develop these effective leadership characteristics.*

*Source:* HMM Leading and Motivating.

TABLE A - 2

## Managing Stress Levels

What bothers the individuals on your team the most about the current changes in your workplace? What are the sources of the stress?

How can you minimize or eliminate the excess stress?

\_\_\_\_ Give advance warning, minimize surprises

\_\_\_\_ Encourage the sharing of information

\_\_\_\_ Foster a sense of humor in the workplace

\_\_\_\_ Reassess/reassign work tasks to balance workloads

\_\_\_\_ Recognize feelings and encourage members to express them

What sources of support (including peer or supervisory support) can you enlist to help manage stress levels?

List each member of your team. What are each member's prevailing emotions right now? Identify ways in which you can respond to each team member.

| Team Member | Status/Symptoms | Ways to Respond |
|---|---|---|
| | | |
| | | |
| | | |
| | | |
| | | |
| | | |
| | | |
| | | |
| | | |

*Source:* HMM Capitalizing on Change.

**TABLE A - 3**

## Focus and Synergy

| Obstacle to Team's Progress | Options for Overcoming the Obstacle | Rank the Options (1 most promising, 5 least promising) | Allies, Resources, Special Training |
|---|---|---|---|
| | | | |
| | | | |
| | | | |
| | | | |
| | | | |
| | | | |
| | | | |
| | | | |
| | | | |
| | | | |
| | | | |
| | | | |
| | | | |

*Source:* HMM Capitalizing on Change.

**TABLE A - 4**

## Gathering and Sharing Information

When was the last time you updated team members about the latest developments in the current change process? What were their specific concerns?

List the most significant new initiatives currently under way for the company as a whole, your division or unit, and your individual team.

What are the major rumors now running through the organization? What information about each can you share with your team?

What is the best way of making this information relevant to your team (e.g., one-on-one meeting, general meeting, memo)?

| Development/Rumor/Initiative | Method | Timing |
|---|---|---|
|  |  |  |

*Source:* HMM Capitalizing on Change.

# Notes

## Chapter 1

1.  Michael Beer and Nitin Nohria, "Cracking the Code of Change," *Harvard Business Review* 78, no. 3 (May–June 2000): 133–141.

2.  American Management Association, "1993 Survey on Downsizing," (New York: American Management Association, 1993), 3.

3.  Beer and Nohria, "Cracking the Code of Change," 134–135.

4.  Dave Ulrich, *Human Resource Champions* (Boston: Harvard Business School Press, 1996), 153.

## Chapter 2

1.  Michael Beer and Nitin Nohria, "Cracking the Code of Change," *Harvard Business Review* 78, no. 3 (May–June 2000): 133–141.

2.  "How to Get Aboard a Major Change Effort: An Interview with John Kotter," *Harvard Management Update,* September 1996.

3.  Michael Beer, Russell A. Eisenstat, and Bert Spector, "Why Change Programs Don't Produce Change," *Harvard Business Review* 68, no. 6 (November–December 1990): 7–12.

4.  Ibid.

5.  John P. Kotter, "Leading Change: Why Transformation Efforts Fail," *Harvard Business Review* 73, no. 2 (March–April 1995): 59–67.

6.  Paul Strebel, "Why Do Employees Resist Change?" *Harvard Business Review* 74, no. 3 (May–June 1996): 86–92.

7.  Adapted from *Realizing Change,* an interactive CD-ROM based on the change literature of John Kotter (Boston, MA: Harvard Business School Publishing, 1997).

8.  Michael Beer, Russell A. Eisenstat, and Bert Spector, *The Critical Path to Corporate Renewal* (Boston, MA: Harvard Business School Press, 1990), 184–201.

9.  Ibid., 202.

10.  Robert H. Schaffer and Harvey A. Thomson, "Successful Change

Programs Begin with Results," *Harvard Business Review* 70, no. 1 (January–February 1992): 80–89.

11. The SQA story is told in David Bovet and Joseph Martha, *Value Nets* (New York: John Wiley & Sons, Inc., 2000), 169–182.

12. Everett M. Rogers, *Diffusion of Innovation,* 3rd edition (New York: The Free Press, 1983), 5.

## Chapter 3

1. Eric Hoffer, *The Ordeal of Change* (Cutchogue, NY: Buccaneer Books, 1976), 3.

2. See the Myers-Briggs Type Indicator®, Consulting Psychologists Press, Inc.

3. See W. Christopher Musselwhite and Robyn Ingram, *Change Style Indicator* (Greensboro, NC: The Discovery Learning Press, 1999).

4. Ibid., 4.

5. Paul R. Lawrence, "How to Deal With Resistance to Change," *Harvard Business Review* XLVII (January–February 1969): 4–12, 166–176.

6. Robert Kegan and Lisa Laskow Lahey, "The Real Reason People Won't Change," *Harvard Business Review* 79, no. 10 (November 2001): 84–92.

7. Everett M. Rogers, *Diffusion of Innovation,* 3rd ed. (New York: The Free Press, 1983) 315–316.

## Chapter 4

1. Laurence Barton, *Crisis in Organizations II* (Cincinnati: Southwestern College Publishing Company, 2001), 8.

2. Richard Boudreaux, "Putin Says He Will Take Complete Responsibility for Kursk Disaster," *Los Angeles Times*, 24 August 2000.

3. Barton, *Crisis*, 2.

## Chapter 5

1. Larry Alexander, "Successfully Implementing Strategic Decisions," *Long Range Planning* 18, no. 3 (1985): 91–97.

2. Michael L. Tushman and Charles A. O'Reilly III, *Winning through Innovation* (Boston, MA: Harvard Business School Press, 1997), 190.

3. John F. Kotter, *Leading Change* (Boston, MA: Harvard Business School Press, 1996).

4. This section leans heavily on Todd Jick, "Implementing Change," Class note 9-491-114 (Boston: Harvard Business School, 1991).

5. John Kotter, "Leading Change: Why Transformation Efforts Fail," *Harvard Business Review* 73, no. 2 (March–April 1995): 66.

6. Adapted from Rebecca Saunders, "Communicating Change," *Harvard Management Communication Letter,* August 1999.

7. Michael Beer and Nitin Nohria, "Cracking the Code of Change," *Harvard Business Review* 78, no. 3 (May–June 2000): 137.

## Chapter 6

1. Harry Woodward and Steve Bucholz, *Aftershock* (New York: John Wiley & Sons, Inc., 1987).

2. Adapted from Todd D. Jick, "Note on the Recipients of Change," Note 9-491-039 (Boston: Harvard Business School, 1990, revised 1996).

3. Ken Hultmans, *The Path of Least Resistance* (Austin, TX: Learning Concepts, 1979).

## Chapter 7

1. Paul Argenti, "Crisis Communication: Lessons from 9/11," *Harvard Business Review,* December 2002, 103–109.

2. Ibid., 103–109.

## Chapter 8

1. Chris Zook and Darrell Rigby, "How to Think Strategically in a Recession," *Harvard Management Update,* November 2001, 8–9.

# *About the Subject Advisers*

**MIKE BEER** is Cahners-Rabb Professor of Business Administration, Emeritus, at the Harvard Business School, where he still teaches in the areas of organizational effectiveness, human resource management, and organizational change. Prior to joining the Harvard faculty, he was Director of Organization Research and Development at Corning, Inc., where he was responsible for stimulating a number of innovations in management. He has authored or coauthored several books and articles. *The Critical Path to Corporate Renewal* (Harvard Business School Press, 1990), which deals with the problems of large-scale corporate change, won the Johnson, Smith, and Knisley Award for the best book in executive leadership in 1991 and was a finalist for the Academy of Management Terry Book Award that year. His most recent book, edited with Nitin Nohria, is *Breaking the Code of Change* (Harvard Business School Press, 2000). In the last several years, Professor Beer has developed and researched a process by which top teams can assess and develop their organization's capability to implement their strategy. He has served on the editorial board of several journals and the board of governors of the Academy of Management, is Chairman of the Center for Organizational Fitness, and has consulted with many Fortune 500 companies.

**LARRY BARTON** is president of The American College, a leader in financial services education based in Bryn Mawr, Pennsylvania, focused on the insurance and financial services industries. Dr. Barton began his career as a journalist, writing for the *Boston Globe, New York Times,* and other publications focusing on corporate debacles; that led to teaching management communications and crisis management at Harvard Business School, Boston College, and Penn State University from 1985 to 1995. Starting in 1987 he began consulting with major companies on crisis prevention and risk management, leading him to join Motorola as vice president of communications and public affairs, where he served from 1995 to 1999. Over the years he has consulted with Exxon Mobil, Disney, Honda, Nike, GoldStar of Korea, and the Japanese Ministry of Information, among many other assignments. He has managed more than three hundred serious incidents for these clients, including work-place murder and executive threats, embezzlement, product tampering, extortion, and various natural disasters.

Dr. Barton is the author of three books, including the best-selling *Crisis in Organizations II*. He is a frequent speaker at insurance and risk management forums on public perceptions of corporations during and after a high-profile incident. He has been featured in the *Wall Street Journal* and has been interviewed by the major global television networks regarding the effective management of crises.

# About the Writer

**RICHARD LUECKE** is the writer of this and eleven other books in the Harvard Business Essentials series. Based in Salem, Massachusetts, Mr. Luecke has authored or developed more than thirty books and dozens of articles on a wide range of business subjects. He has an M.B.A. from the University of St. Thomas.

# MENTORS ON DEMAND

**WHEN YOU'RE A MANAGER,** every day brings fresh challenges. And sometimes, you need a little help finding the right solution for them.

That's where the *Pocket Mentors* come in. Written by experts in the field, these books offer clear, practical advice on everyday problems—from understanding finance to managing crises.

Best of all, you can get these tools right now. Download copies of the most popular *Pocket Mentors* and get instant access to the answers you need, when you need them.

**TO LEARN MORE OR DOWNLOAD POCKET MENTORS, VISIT:**

www.harvardbusiness.org/press